RETAIL IMAGE
& GRAPHIC IDENTITY

RETAIL
IMAGE
& GRAPHIC IDENTITY

Joan G. Salb

Retail Reporting Corporation, New York

51343

659.19
SAL

Retail Reporting Corporation
302 Fifth Avenue
New York, NY 10001

Distributors to the trade in the United States and
Canada:
Van Nostrand Reinhold
115 Fifth Avenue
New York, NY 10003

Distributors outside the United States and Canada:
Hearst Books International
1350 Avenue of the Americas
New York, NY 10019

Library of Congress Cataloging in Publication Data:
Retail Image & Graphic Identity

ISBN 0-934590-62-1

Book Design/Production:
Stephen Bridges
Eilis McDonnell
Jack Boyce
Bobby Hranichny

Printed in Hong Kong

CONTENTS

To my dear husband, Jack,
for more than just his love and
support... for his professional
counsel and his good judgment
as well — all of which have
added to the uniqueness and
quality of my first book.

INTRODUCTION

The simple fact that you have this book in hand indicates your recognition of design as something to be regarded as both aesthetic and pragmatic. Isn't it amazing that many still don't grasp the two-pronged concept… and yet they seem to have survived in this increasingly competitive industry we lovingly call "retail"?

From my perspective, I think such survivors will become fewer and fewer. The trend has already begun.

Some stores are disappearing altogether. And some are merging with others—which increases the image blur. "What is this store that I am in?" asks the customer, as he or she flounders for a credit card or checkbook.

That's not the case at MacKenzie-Childs. Or Oilily. Or at Game Keeper. Or the Forum Shops at Caesars. Or at Universal CityWalk.

That's not the case at the Coyote Cafe. Or Wolfgang Puck's. Or the Russian Tea Room.

That's not the case on Alaska Airlines. On a Princess Cruise. On the Orient Express. At the Marriott Desert Springs Resort and Spa.

Each is extraordinarily identifiable (not only by virtue of intrinsic distinctiveness)—but because design has been utilized and loyally integrated to communicate the image and the essence directly and visually to the consumer.

It was not easy to chapterize this book. Some of my favorite retailers seemed to fit no particular category. Thus the lively chapter titled: "OMNIUM-GATHERUM: A SURPRISING DIVERSITY OF RETAILERS." You'll wish you could buy your art supplies in Tokyo at .TOO. And if your eyeglass prescription needs renewal and you're near West Sussex in England, stop in at Arthur Hayes Optometrists.

The travel and leisure industry has earned a chapter of its own. "RETAIL GETAWAYS" demonstrates the power of visual identity reflected by several hotels . . . as well as an airline, an exotic train and a luxury cruise ship. Interestingly, this industry probably does the best job, over all, of creating visual identity that invites instant recognition by consumers. This kind of familiarity creates loyalties that encourage frequency of purchase.

"FOOD GLORIOUS FOOD" (as you might guess) is a compendium of restaurants with plenty of pizzazz. You must sample this chapter to get the flavor. For sure, you'll wish, at least, that you had a souvenir matchbook from each food retailer.

I separated the coffee bars from the restaurants because this classification has really taken off in these last couple of years. And "COFFEE COFFEE EVERYWHERE" illustrates a few of those who have translated the richness of their own individual coffee house identity through unique, collaborative design and graphics.

This couldn't be a book without some "traditional" fashion stores. Although as you will see, when you read the chapter "FASHION AND SPECIALTY STORES: ABOVE AND BEYOND THE ORDINARY", that there's very little that's traditional. You may never even have heard of some of them. Peaches en Regalia? Nex.is? MacKenzie-Childs? Reviewing the transparencies and information for this chapter was especially difficult and time-consuming because there were so many submissions. But ultimately, the best were culled, leaving behind those whose visual vagueness succeeded only in murking their own fashion-identity waters.

Last but not least… the location where customers might find many of the above-mentioned retailers. "SHOPPING CENTERS: WHAT THE WORLD IS COMING TO." As with submissions of fashion retailers, many of the stories and transparencies I collected were innocuous, enigmatic and without any semblance of retail image or graphic identity. (It's a wonder consumers find their way to some of these malls at all!) But you'll love Superstition Springs and Valencia Mall. And you'll shout "olé" at the visual energy of Rosarito Beach's Festival Plaza.

It's time to take out your box of paper clips and your pad of 3-M stick-'ems. There are sure to be several special pages you'll want to key so you can refer to them easily. The many colorful examples of creativity in design integration will surely spark your own creativity. Moreover, it is our hope that this book may help you make "believers" out of any colleagues who have not yet seen the light. May they come to recognize (as you have) the imperativeness of achieving retail design that's totally collaborative and integrated and that pervades all aspects of a retailer's communications with its public!

Joan G. Salb

FASHION AND SPECIALTY STORES:
above and beyond the ordinary

Forgive us if you don't find any of your old favorites. We love Banana Republic and The Gap and the Body Shop and Ann Taylor as much as you do. But we really did our best to search outside "the familiar" to find as many wonderful shops as we could that would be new news to you!

And search — we did. Our phone calls and faxes to the Netherlands ran up a tidy sum… but we succeeded in collecting for you, the wonderful story of the Oilily children's stores.

A visit to Madison avenue was fortuitous — as we encountered the one, the only MacKenzie-Childs store, where imagination reigns and identity conveys its royal presence.

We journeyed to Kobe, Japan where the strength of Sanyo's striking identity program has helped it achieve a dominant role in the department store business.

Though all categories of retailers are struggling to achieve that all-important recognizable image — probably none is more challenged than those who feature "fashion." From my perspective, I often liken their campaigns and images to auto companies: as soon as someone comes out with a new look, others follow suit and then they all look the same.

None of the retailers in this chapter look the same! We think you'll find them original, imaginative and entertaining. In addition, perhaps you'll find some inspiration in their ideas (which is in part, the objective of this very first volume on retail image and graphic identity.)

OILILY

The Netherlands

Looking at the world from a child's perspective: that is what Oilily is all about. This is a company that has distinguished itself by creating — not child-size versions of grownup clothes, but rather, kid-preferred colorful, imaginative clothing. Fabulous fabrics, wonderfully exuberant prints, incredible color mixes and funny and ingenious details — all combine to make Oilily universally appealing to children.

Everything mixes and matches — as free-wheeling in attitude as the non-stop energy of the children themselves. And all of this play and mingling of color is communicated the moment a customer comes upon an Oilily store. Store design (both exterior and interior), inviting display windows and enchanting visual merchandising capture and communicate the essence of Oilily in an instant.

Oilily's imagery is infectiously dispatched on wrapping paper, shopping bags, packaging (especially the charming children's cosmetics and perfumes), in-store signage, tags, labels, catalogs, calendars and even fun-filled Oilily magazines.

With a clear understanding that nothing is subject to change as quickly as a child's world, Oilily resists succumbing to outside trends or fashions. With more than 2000 outlets in 36 countries, the company has one very singular identity. And no matter what surprising variations are created — it remains totally recognizable.

New York Retail Store Design:
Kiku Obata & Company, New York
Art Direction:
Denise van Poppel, de Stores bv, Oilily,
  The Netherlands
Graphics:
Margot Vos, Jean Philipse, de Studio bv, Oilily,
  The Netherlands

OILILY

The Netherlands

This very unique personality has resulted in Oilily becoming part of the vernacular in some parts of the world — like Oilily children, Oilily neighborhoods, Oilily villages. The best comment of all sums it up: Oilily happiness.

NEX·IS

Singapore

Everything about Nex·is (an offshoot of the CK Tang department store) conveys a sense of funky, fashionable unpredictability. Even the name was created to form a sense of anticipation; it is an abbreviation of "the next thing is . . ."

With the name as the first note of the rhythm for the design of this store for the youth market of Singapore, everything from signage to shoe boxes has been designed to keep the beat going.

The factors that influenced the graphics for Nex·is came from the street culture and fashion which play an influential role in the lives of the retailer's target audience of young men and women. All kinds of symbols that typify that genre have been graphically employed — cleverly seeming almost haphazard (but clearly arranged). Images of VW Beetles along with flowers and fruit are mixed with icons from Singaporean culture.

In counterpoint to these wildly artful images, the Nex·is logo is serious, strong and dramatic. It dominates wherever it appears — having already achieved a high degree of recognizability. As well as external and internal signage, a full range of innovative and unusual packaging geared to the youth market was developed. There are shopping bags and wrapping paper, roll-top packs for socks, shirt banding and a fold-up pyramid. Most fun of all are the shoe boxes with rope handles — which are stacked in depth in the store to create a visual design wall of their own.

The energy of Nex·is design is an accurate reflection of the pace and tempo of its audience — successfully creating an identity that is clearly memorable and in step with the customers it wants to woo.

Interior Design and Retail Graphics: Fitch, London, England
Photographers: Lewis Mulatero, Kerry Wilson, Jon O'Brien

PEACHES EN REGALIA

Aspen, Colorado

It's classy, it's classic, it's sophisticated. It's Peaches en Regalia. No "cute boutique" here. Owner/designer Patricia Straight has translated her years in fashion design and fashion modeling into a pair of chic shops in Aspen, Colorado and Del Mar, California.

The concept of white walls with accents of pale peach and natural were fastidiously selected to be subtle enough to enhance the merchandise yet distinctive enough to identify the personality of the store. The addition of grey and black emerged when the decision was made to add a men's classification to the already-successful women's line.

The name, Peaches en Regalia, and the design of the logo/type face were also integral parts of contriving a fashion identity that would be distinctive. Only the most intimate customers know that a Frank Zappa song from the 60's inspired the name. No matter, it has a special,

somewhat-European intrigue about it. Besides the abbreviation of Peaches en Regalia as "PR", it is interesting to note those are also initials of the owner (Patricia) and her son (Ryan). To some, the handsome selection of type might seem reminiscent of "Rolls Royce" — and though, not the intent, the parallelism is definitely appropriate.

Peaches en Regalia is commited to putting its identity wherever possible. Wonderful woven labels are sewn into both men's and women's garments. And even clothing hangers bear the PR logo. Gift boxes and shopping bags carry a special cache — both peach and grey are available with shiny embossed silver or gold stickers and bows.

There's a certain timelessness in the integrated design program of Peaches en Regalia — one that provides a continuity in establishing a very recognizable identity.

Architect: *Wedum & Associates, Architect, Inc., Aspen, CO*
Store Concept and Graphic Design: *Patricia Straight*
Photographer: *Reed Kaestner, Del Mar, CA*

TRAIL MARK

Minneapolis, Minnesota

Wind, water, earth and sky. The elements of the great outdoors set the parameters for the architectural design of the Trail Mark stores, for the visual merchandising and for the comprehensive and collaborative graphic identity program.

From the moment a consumer approaches the distinctive facade of a Trail Mark store and walks into the coalescing urban and rustic environment — through the entire shopping experience, there is not one iota of ambiguity as to store identification.

The entryway to Trail Mark is beneath a pivoting overhead "garage" door of steel and corrugated fiberglass. A bed of washed river rock is the threshold. And flanking the access is a column of huge logs — stacked one atop the other. The storefront window (upon which is etched the longitude and latitude of the store) is supported by an outcropping of rock.

Above the entry, the Trail Mark logo commands attention. It is a striking composition of the twigs and stones used to mark trails. And this logo, along with these same raw materials are repeated everywhere — bringing together a retailer's otherwise disparate ingredients into a unified statement. Shelf markers imitate trail markers. Customers carry merchandise away in twig-handled brown paper "feed bags". And, with relentless consistency, the Trail Mark logo conveys the store's identity — not only on collateral, but frequently on merchandise which is displayed on tables made of tree branches or shelves supported by canoe paddles.

Please pardon the pun but Trail Mark's design identity program has left no stone unturned!

THEY'RE NOT STONEWASHED.

(WE FIGURE THEY'LL SEE ENOUGH
ROCKS AFTER YOU BUY THEM.)

*[Columbia Tough Mother™
relaxed-fit jeans, $32]*

Columbia's Bio-wash finishing method gives Tough Mother

jeans a smoother color than stonewashing, with no abrasion of

seams or stitching. The result is a stylin' pair of jeans that can

stand up to almost anything your legs can dish out.

TRAIL MARK

Architect/Interior Design: Shea Architects, Inc., Minneapolis, MN
Gregory Rothweiler, Design Director
Julie Oseld, Project Architect
Graphic Design Firm: *Duffy, Inc, Minneapolis, MN*
Photographer: *George Heinrich*

GOODNEST

Minneapolis, Minnesota

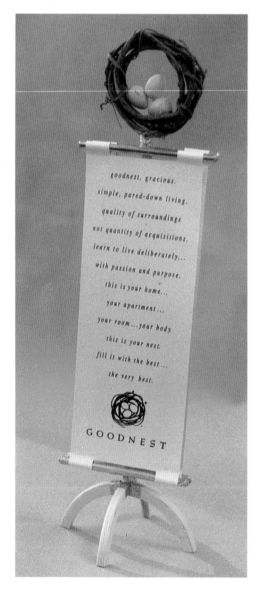

Although this is not a stand-alone store, Goodnest earns its place in our book as a retailer that has imaginatively translated the underlying concept of a natural gifts "shop" into a totally integrated image program.

Paying close heed to the merchandising planned for select Dayton-Hudson and Marshall Field's stores, the designers envisioned the shop as an environment where birch-bark baskets, pine rocking chairs, organic skin care and unbleached sheets would sit comfortably together.

First step: to create a name and logo that would embody the concept and communicate the message to consumers. Thus, "Goodnest" — a symbol for goodness, simplicity and quality. Goodnest is about feathering one's nest. And the striking logo says just that in an instant.

Goodnest fixtures were designed to show off the merchandise. But, at the same time, they were ingeniously constructed of materials and elements that kept the visual identity strongly in the forefront. Lightly varnished natural woods were chosen, along with copper inlay signing and trim as well as unbleached canvas banners and banner brackets topped with birds' nests and wooden eggs.

There's strength in the quietness and neutralness of the Goodnest design. But the graphic identity is not shy about speaking its message. And more than that, it speaks (literally) the actual words of nutritional experts, naturalists, philosophers and writers. Customers enjoy quotes on the benefits of diet, aromatherapy, exercise and gardening as well as the poetic messages of Thoreau and Dickinson.

An interesting postscript: a Goodnest line of bath and shower products has been chosen to be showcased at the Smithsonian Museum in Washington, D.C. as an exemplary example of eco-sensitive packaging.

Designer: Adrienne Weiss Corporation, Chicago, IL
Photographer: Todd Sharkey Photography

MAC KENZIE-CHILDS, LTD.

Aurora, New York

To understand the extraordinary presentation of the MacKenzie-Childs flagship store in New York City and how it came to be, you must first know something about the life force of the company itself: Victoria and Richard MacKenzie-Childs. Both are formally trained artists whose early experimentation with design in theater, fabric, clothing and costumes, coupled with an invaluable year at an English pottery factory, set the stage for launching a business based on the ceramic wares they had lovingly crafted for home, friends and family.

It is this very personal quality that pervades the company and creates their unique image and identity. Merchandising and marketing both radiate the same message of a fresh, pure, colorful, homespun culture. There's a celebration and a jubilation in the store design, the shopping bag design, stationery, promotion pieces and portfolios — exactly the same joyful expression that's conveyed through the merchandise.

Spirited handmade furnishings, glassware, linen, specialized accessories like ceramic tassels… and the company's signature — the majolica dinnerware — all come together within a stunning theatrical environment. It is impossible to pass the storefront without

stopping. Bold striped pennants with ceramic tassels frame the front and second floor canopies. Both outside and inside, perky pink geraniums (and a second story balcony with flower-filled terra-cotta pots) arrest the attention of Madison Avenue strollers.

Inside the store, splashes of color and texture, ribbons and roses, fringed valances, pottery and hand-painted tiles that decorate floors, walls and ceilings — all combine to showcase the merchandise and create a fanciful atmosphere.

If MacKenzie-Childs seems more like "home" than "store" … it is their philosophy of life that provides this disarming freshness and spontaneity of image.

Architect: *Victoria and Richard MacKenzie-Childs*
Store Design and Graphics: *Victoria and Richard MacKenzie-Childs*
Photographer: *Nan Melville*

ACA JOE

Perisur Mall, Mexico City, Mexico

Mexico City is an important center of culture and fashion. And a growing number of American retailers have come to recognize the potential of that marketplace. From this perspective, Aca Joe decided it was important to create an entirely new store prototype for the Mexican market.

The store was to feature an expanded line of fashion-oriented clothing and accessories. It was to look sophisticated but not expensive… comfortable but not too casual. And above all, Aca Joe wanted the store to have a distinctive American feeling which would appeal to the Mexican consumers' passion for U.S. fashion yet not overshadow their Latino loyalty.

Ole! A stunningly simple almost Shaker-like American haberdashery. Extensive use of maple with cherry accents provide a clean, modern masculine look. Wall displays and free-standing fixtures continue the uncluttered, comtemporary image. In deference to the host country, Mexican tiles are used as contrasting accents in the planked floor design.

Though the choice was made to employ many of the visual merchandising techniques as well as the integrated signage and graphics which had been used successfully in American mall stores, great care has been taken that these translations avoid any direct references to the U.S.

The most dominant symbol is the bold diamond shaped Aca Joe logo. The word "original" placed beneath the name communicates the authenticity of this men's American fashion retailer. This logo is used extensively in all graphics and signage as well as on stationery and promotion pieces. We see Aca Joe labels on merchandise, logos on shopping bags and boxes — even on wooden hangers.

Design Firm: *SDI-HTI (Cincinnati)*
Design Principal: *Joan Donnelly*
Store Designer: *Beth Neroni*
Graphic Designer: *Tim Frame*
Architects: *Jay Kratz & Bill Bily*
Photographer: *Alessandro Gamboa*

DEBENHAMS

Like the immediate recognizability of McDonald's golden-arched "M", Britain's Debenhams is aiming at making their big "D" an identifiable symbol for department store shoppers. The enormous stylized, multi-colored letter beckons from the entryway of the Debenham store. It makes an emphatic statement and provides an attractive invitation to step inside and shop.

The new identity initial and its accompanying contemporized logo typography comprise the first visual strategies in Debenham's redesign. Equally important is the physical refurbishment; store facade and interior architectural design have been given a major facelift to reflect the retailer's commitment to providing customers with both updated merchandising and a contemporary shopping environment.

Characterizing the redefinition of Debenhams is an avid attention to the use of contemporary materials. Natural woods and subtle finishes dominate throughout the store. Even the well-known "cosmetics hall" has relinquished its fickle glitz to a look of substance, sophistication and quality.

Great attention has been given to the redesign of signage systems and point-of-sale material.

New private label packaging has been created along with an eye-catching big "D" shopping bag. All aspects of visual communication have been employed to reestablish the image of Debenhams as the leading department store in the U.K. — earning the design team an "A" rating for their "D."

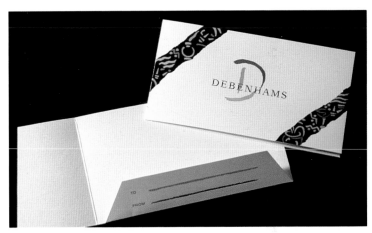

Interior Design and Retail Graphics: Fitch, London, England
Photographer: Tim Hill

29

CHILDREN'S WORLD

London, England

This smart retailer recognized that there were two target audiences to please: the parents and the children. And what more innovative way to address this challenge than to divide the entrance of the store into two components: a real doorway for the grown-ups and a slide for the children!

Yes, Children's World is fun. It is an environment that projects the vitality and spirit of childhood. Everywhere the customer sees the bright primary colors and energetic graphics.

And, since first impressions do count, the front entry of the store was designed to capture the immediate attention of passers-by. The main theme of the storefront is the Children's World totem — a dominant architectural form that has been integrated as a graphic theme on signage, ticketing and also on staff uniforms.

A strategic layout and color-coded graphics system defines each category and specialist concessions, making the store easy to shop. Through-out the store, aisles of vertically stacked shelves achieve identity by their appropriately-colored end-aisle totems. And the aisles have been made wide enough to accommodate baby carriages and shopping baskets. The shopping baskets, by the way, have not been left to chance either: they're colorfully painted, repeating the bright reds, yellows and blues of the design theme.

For young families, Children's World is not only an inviting place to shop, it is a store with a strong visual identity and a memorable retail image.

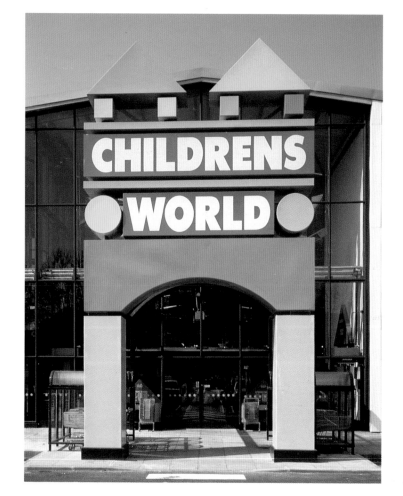

Interior Design and Retail Graphics: *Fitch, Inc., London, England*

Interior Design and Retail Graphics: *Fitch, London, England*
Photographer: *S. Reynolds*

Would Woodhouse be the store for you if you were either a sophisticated, luxury-oriented gentleman of 35 or older… or if you were a younger, upbeat customer? Amazingly, the design team has been able to create a visual atmosphere for Woodhouse that can appeal to both customers.

Shape, color and texture of interior design materials set the stage for this dual-market retailer. The overall color is a strong blue — vibrant but yet in keeping with a "private club" look. It remains a consistent element in both the front section of the store — which has been designed to reflect more of the conservative and formal attitude — as well as in the energetic atmosphere designated in the younger customer's section. It is worth noting that the "rhythm" of the store changes, but the attitude remain constant in both locations.

The deep blue (almost a purple blue) makes a major statement, not only via the store's interior design, but also in terms of the program of graphic identity. This is the corporate color for all printed materials, from shopping bags and boxes to personal bill presentation wallets. And it is made even more recognizable by the very distinctive Woodhouse logo. Interestingly, the logo itself (like the duality of the store) manages to communicate both contemporary flair (the sweeping "W") in tandem with an affluent, professional character (the classic, reserved typestyle).

TAKASHIMAYA

New York, New York

Sh-h-h. The quiet elegance of Takashimaya makes you feel you want to speak in refined, hushed tones. The image is complete and replete with textures, finishes, colorations, design details and furnishings that spell elegance with a capital "E".

Interestingly the essence of the image comes — not from one theme, but rather, from a stunning blending of elements of the 20's, 30's, 40's and 50's with a touch of Regency and a taste of Japanese. It's a toast to glamour. No doubt, Hollywood's legendary Carol Lombard would surely have found an appropriate chaise lounge on which to recline at Takashimaya.

Customers experience the grandeur of the building both from the outside (the 3-story windowed entrance facade is articulated with abstract interpretations of classical architecture)… and from the inside, where an atrium space soars three stories high to reveal a gold-leaf ceiling.

Throughout the floors and departments of Takashimaya, the neutral palette of creams, beiges, browns and blacks (with tiny dashes of red) plays a major role in tying everything together. These colors carry through on the entire range of Takashimaya packaging — a most important ingredient for the store's upscale clientele, whose expectations for

"presentation" are high. Boxes and shopping bags are divinely creamy and glossy — with an understated Takashimaya logo. Rich metallic gold silk tassels and colored tissue add an extra special touch.

Takashimaya has been designed to make a quiet impact on its customers but there's no doubt that the message of luxury is heard loudly and clearly!

Architects: *John Burgee Architects, New York, NY*
Interior Design and Architecture: *Larry Laslo Design Inc., New York, NY*
Graphics: *Susan Slover Design, New York, NY*
Photographer: *Dursten Saylor*

GIANFRANCO LOTTI

If we saw the Mona Lisa winking, we'd surely do a double take. It is this kind of whimsy that invites customers to take a second look at all of Gianfranco Lotti's visual communications. Using a masterful array of re-interpreted Renaissance paintings and tapestries, the design team has integrated the store's classic merchandise within the artwork as if it legitimately belonged there.

These playful images have been strategically created to reinforce the character of Lotti merchandise: quality leather goods and accessories crafted in the finest Florentine tradition and yet styled with clean, classic

shapes. The old paintings appear on bags, boxes, shopping bags, gift tags and hand tags. The warm palette of the Renaissance paintings complement the handsome leather products.

Even the design of the Gianfranco Lotti logo manages to marry the touch of "old" with a contemporary flair. This logo is found richly stamped on the leather goods as well as on all the collateral.

The idea of adopting masterworks from a century renowned for its elegance is indeed very appropriate for this status retailer's communications program. But what takes it out of the ordinary… what makes it recognizable and memorable is the unexpected use of humor. Handled with subtlety and sophistication, this image campaign represents the best of what retail identification is all about.

Design: *Melinda Maniscalco, Pentagram Designs, San Francisco, CA*

THE NATURE COMPANY

Berkeley, California

The Nature Company is certainly not a new store. In fact, its origins date back to 1973. However, this retailer earns a place in our book because, even in the span of two decades, it has never waivered in reinforcing its very distinctive image and identity.

A clear and definitive philosophy guides the design of merchandise and, simultaneously, establishes the tone for the store design and graphics design. Everything fits the heading of paraphernalia for the naturalist. And though some products are serious and some are fun… some are expensive, some inexpensive, there are no shortcuts in the high design level of packaging, labelling and in-store signing.

The rabbit "mascot" is, of course, the most recognizable visual element — appearing on storefronts, on the catalog, on T-shirts and featured on the aprons worn by store associates. He usually appears as an integral part of The Nature Company's logo… but sometimes he stands alone, as in the case of a craftily designed gift picnic box.

The interior layout of each Nature Company store achieves a kind of disorganized organization. The well-conceived clutter makes a visit to the store a "happening". And to enhance the environment, besides the visual clues, Nature Company stores add audio. Piped over the air are the sounds of nature — everything from the ocean to distant thunder. Originally intended only for atmosphere, customer demand resulted in creating a "for-sale" series of the tapes and packaging them with special graphics.

It is admirable that The Nature Company, though expanding worldwide, has been able to carefully manage and maintain its retail image and identity.

Graphic Design: *Pentagram Design, Inc., San Francisco, CA*

DI MAASI SHOEWEAR UNLIMITED

Birmingham, Alabama

When a footwear superstore measures more than 18,000 square feet, carries over 750 footwear styles and features the most popular lines of shoes available for men, women and children … it is quite a challenge to establish an identity of its own — one that will supersede the brand names on display.

To solve this problem, the design team created a strong "umbrella" graphic program which has succeeded in providing the necessary continuity.

Shopping bags, shoe boxes, wall posters and shelf signs feature a variety of jumping feet images. Different feet, different genders, different action poses — but all conveying the attitude of upbeat, smart styling and varied merchandise. These signature graphics charge the store with energy, visual excitement and a slightly European sensibility. Most importantly, they serve to unify the

various shoes areas, bringing them together as shops-within-the-shop.

The bags, boxes and signage also feature the very dynamic DiMassi logo. Presented horizontally at the entryway and vertically within the store, the logo all but jumps at you (just the way the feet do) … spelling its name

in bold black and white with a startling bright red triangle replacing the "A".

Consumers may choose any brand or shoe style at this exciting retail store, but they will never forget: they bought it at DiMassi!

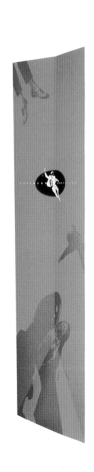

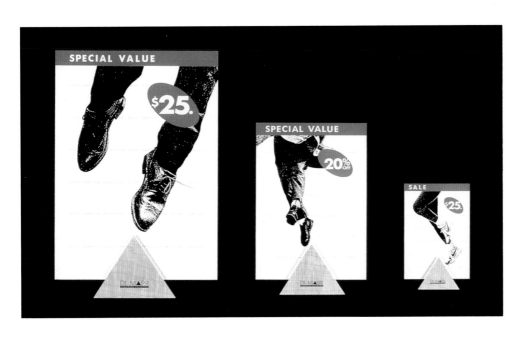

Interior Designer & Graphic Designer:
SDI-HTI, Los Angeles, CA
Photographer: Lewis Kennedy

CLARK'S

London, England

Design Firm: *Kit Henrichs, Pentagram Designs, San Francisco, CA*

Who are those funny fellows? Why, they're Cyrus and James — the Clark brothers. What better way to give a store an exclusive identification than to use spokesmen that no other retailer could lay claim to. And so, the design team has gone back 150 years and breathed life into the company's founders.

Though Clark's is well-known in England, its expansion into America and other parts of the world necessitated a unique marketing and graphic program to create high awareness. Appearing as something halfway between a tintype and a cartoon, the siblings are becoming as recognizable as the Smith Brothers! They stand rigidly, carrying a stiff

Union Jack flag — seeming to rise out of a "life saver" that carries the caption "Clark's Originals."

This design element has been used frequently within the retail setting. It appears as part of the display fixturing and it pops up, amusingly, at numerous point-of-purchase locations. Accents of red and blue (colors from the United Kingdom flag) add to the continuity of the visual merchandising.

The Clark Brothers also makes their presence known to consumers outside the store. Relentlessly reminding consumers to "forget-us-not", Cyrus and James follow along on all the shoe boxes as well as on direct mail pieces and promotional literature.

By endowing the storename with the personality of the original proprietors, Clark's has established a most distinctive identity… at the same time, infusing the business of "shoes" with a memorable, jocular image.

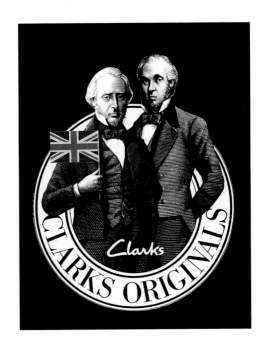

RENEE STEVENS

Massapequa, New York

With so much copycat-ing in the arena of contemporary store design of women's fashion boutiques, it's no surprise that some customers find store identities seem to overlap.

Not the case at Renee Stevens. This retailer has clearly made its name and personality known and identifiable and has successfully positioned itself as a value-oriented women's separates store with a fashionable, upscale attitude. Both the store's environment and its smart graphics design program give Renee Stevens a distinctive image.

The dominant graphic design element is the curve — "the ultimate feminine form." This curve motif forms the defining component in the creation of the brand-name logo itself.

This logo — which is both graceful and strong at the same time, makes itself known everywhere in the store display and signage. Further, it is repeated on shopping bags and stationery. Also, it is used extensively on all packaging and labeling: hangtags and sewn-in labels, keeping Renee Stevens clearly top-of-mind even in customers' closets!

Interior Design and Graphics Program:

GRID International, Inc., New York (formerly International Design Group)

44

Can there be anyplace in the world where one cannot pause and refresh with a Coca-Cola? The familiar taste and the familiar identity of Coke cross borders, rivers, continents.

And on Fifth Avenue in New York, the Coca-Cola Company has a special presence: a shop that celebrates Coca-Cola with the most colorful array of Coca-Cola logo merchandise — set within an environment that has been designed to capture the essence of the company's image.

Architecturally, the store's floor plan makes the first "statement": the 150-foot long store is shaped like a "C"! Customers are enticed to walk the distance of the store by the unique illuminated pathway. The flooring, itself, has been designed to communicate the effervescence of the Coca-Cola carbonation:

the theme of "bubbles" is presented through the texture mix of terrazzo and stainless steel.

The ceiling design (like the flooring) has been created to reflect the Coca-Cola identity. Mimicking the shifting, ribbon-like script of the name's logo, the ceiling is also a "ribbon". In white and silver, it is not only structurally shaped to undulate, but a theatrically-controlled lighting system puts the ribbon "in motion".

Scattered throughout the Coca-Cola store are archival exhibits, antique reproductions, photos and historic memorabilia. In addition, there's a 15-screen video wall and an interactive video, housed in a giant Coca-Cola can. Within this most imaginative environment, customers will find an exhaustive collection of Coca-Cola merchandise — for wearing, for carrying, for collecting!

Architect: *Ronnette Riley Architect, New York, NY*
Principal: *Ronnette Riley, AIA*
Project Architect: *Dale Linden Turner, AIA*
Graphics: *Ronnette Riley Architect/Real Design*
Principal: *Ronnette Riley, AIA*
Project Director: *Margot Perman*
Photographer: *Otto Baitz, Freehold, NJ*

LIZ CLAIBORNE

New York, New York

Just say "Liz". Everyone knows you're referring to one of the THE names in sportswear. As a major vendor in the department store business, Liz Claiborne surprised no one when the company entered the retail world with its own stores.

Having achieved its strong consumer following through the language of its styling, Liz Claiborne had also established a distinctive image through its graphic program. It is these graphic images and themes that set the foundation for the architectural design and interior design of the Liz Claiborne stores.

The company's signature red, yellow and blue colors had originally evolved because those were the favorite colors of Liz, herself. Faithful to that palette, these colors have been integrated into various elements of store interior design. Sometimes on columns, sometimes on chairs — but always in a strategic location where they could be viewed without interference from possibly conflicting colored merchandise.

Working in counterpoint to the color accents, the overall material for store design is natural materials (mostly woods) which are neutral, contemporary and straightforward — a distinctly architectural translation of the essence of Liz Claiborne fashion.

It also should be mentioned that environmental concerns dictate which woods may or may not be used. No mahogany, teak or rosewood: a statement opposing the deforestation of the world's rain forests.

As important as the Liz Claiborne signature colors are the signature shapes. Already, the packaging for Liz fragrance has become instantly identifiable. The triangle form is used as stationery logo, on shopping bags — even frequently as dimensional merchandise display units.

Architects: *Brand+Allen Architects, Inc., Houston, Texas*
SDI-HTI, New York, N.Y.
Photographer: *Peter Paige*

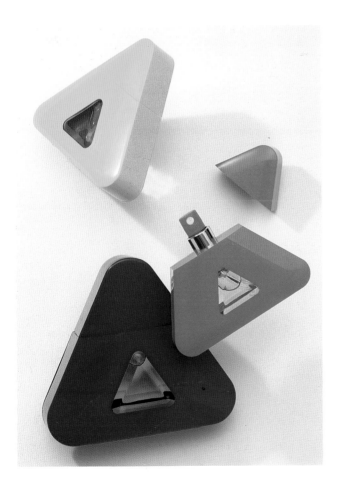

SANYO DEPARTMENT STORE

Kobe, Japan

The architecture of the almost-white stone facade of the building makes a dramatic introduction to this fine Japanese department store. The distinctive, linear Sanyo name is dimensionalized and raised off the stone surface. The colors are fresh and clean against the white: the letters are finished in marine blue and the tapered, curved arch above them are nile green. Sanyo flags fly in the breeze, giving the building an important global, almost "official" look.

The blue, green and white colors, along with the logo itself, combine to serve as the dominant graphic elements. For all packaging, wrapping and shopping bags used by the store, a wide brush-stroke of marine blue is rendered on the diagonal— sweeping from dense blue to dry brush-stroke. The Sanyo name appears in white, crowned by the green arc above it. For variety, sometimes the colors are used in reverse or in different order. But the logo and look never stray from the core concept.

Stationery, I.D. cards, promotion collateral (as well as much of the merchandise) carry the Sanyo logo, reinforcing the store's identity and smart, contemporary image.

Design Firm: *Profile Design, San Francisco, CA*
Architect/Art Director: *Konichi Nishiwaki*

HANNA-BARBERA

Los Angeles, California

Scooby dooby doo! That's Flintstones language. And it means "hooray". My sentiments, exactly, regarding the Hanna-Barbera retail stores.

A visit is a delightful diversion; the store design features bright colors, playful imagery and wacky humor to recreate the whimsical world of cartoons. It's an environment that captures the spirit of many different animated characters — in sight, sound and motion. On the shelves: a wide variety of signature merchandise: toys, games, plush dolls, clothing, toys, novelties, books, records, jewelry and artwork.

The contemporary design of the Hanna-Barbera store unites prehistoric elements from The Flintstones' world and futuristic gadgetry from The Jetsons' universe. For example, the facade combines boulders from Bedrock (The Flintstones' hometown) with a space-age antenna direct from The Jetsons' Orbit City. Inside, customers follow a central aisle which is paved with pebbled tiles to resemble a cartoon roadway in Bedrock. Above the aisle, a cartoon sky is dotted with fluffy cartoon clouds.

Signage and end aisle displays are not mere placards; they are cartoon creations. Even the door frames and TV screen frames are shaped and colored to represent the giddy environment. Instead of one shopping bag design, there are several — each depicting a different cartoon character.

Audio-visual effects are an added dimension to the environment: there's a video jukebox, an interactive video laser disc system and a number of video screens. The popularity of the Hanna-Barbera creations on TV and on film is a constant reinforcement for the retail stores — and vice-versa!

Architect, Interior Designer, Graphics
Designer: *SDI-HTI, Cincinnati, OH*
Photographer: *Paul Bielenberg*

DOLE

Dole Cannery Square, Dole Logo Shop, Dole Kids Store
Honolulu, Hawaii

Project Concept:

Arnold C. Savrann, AIA, Castle and Cooke
    Properties, Inc.

Interior Architecture & Graphic Design:

Charles K.C. Lau, AIA, Brian Takahashi, AIA,
AM Partners, Inc., Honolulu, HI

Photographer: David Franzen

The Dole retail identity story requires a niche of its own — because it expresses itself in three different manifestations: the Dole Logo Shop, the Dole Kids Store and the Dole Cannery Shopping Mall.

The original Dole plantation cannery served as the inspiration for this trio of retail environments. When tours of the pineapple cannery were phased out, the building sought a purpose of its own. Space-wise, location-wise, it held enormous promise as a retail center. The result: a village of historic plantation shops that is a true reflection of Dole's presence in Hawaii. Both the overall mall design and individual storefronts convey a unified visual image. Pineapple logo marquis signs articulate the theme. Everything is rendered in bold plantation colors.

The mainstays of the Dole identity are the two Dole retail stores.

The Dole Logo Shop cleverly takes its cue from the industrial complex that once was. Large concrete columns, catwalks and industrial handrails set the stage. Everything is painted stark white — a subtle framework for the enormously colorful Dole logo merchandise. Canvas bags, sweatshirts, sweaters, caps, shorts, socks, fresh produce ties, cookbooks, watches, luggage tags, gold ball packs, etc. Dole graphic signage is prominently displayed everywhere.

Just a few steps away is the Dole Kids Store. Colorful and whimsical in design, it reiterates its heritage with the recreation of a plantation train station for kids. The bright yellow Dole choo-choo rides along the make-believe vinyl track. The cashier's desk resembles a train ticket booth. Pineapple motifs along with logo and theme merchandise combine to articulate the Dole identity.

WHAT THE WORLD IS COMING TO:
shopping centers

Everybody comes to the shopping center. To shop. To catch a movie. To dine. To ice skate. To ride the carousel. To attend a special event. To take a workshop. To hear a speaker. To meet a movie star. Or, merely, to stroll around and experience the energy and excitement of the bustling crowds.

Shopping centers and malls are destination centers. They are places that consumers choose to go. And "choose" is the operative word because proliferation of malls and renovation of earlier centers have expanded the options for shoppers, once they get behind the wheels of their cars.

What's another couple of miles if there's a shopping center that's different and worth the trip? And, on the other hand, how about the joy of shopping "downtown", where developers have breathed new life into the city by revitalizing the urban mall?

How does a consumer recognize and remember which is which? Aha — that's what image and identity is all about. That's the essence of creating the proverbial "top-of-mind" aware-ness. And in our chapter on shopping centers and malls, we've selected the most amazing mix of malls — each one with its own personality and character.

So distinctive is each "story", we promise, you'll feel as if you've made the trip yourself — kind of a virtual reality journey to Lille, France or Las Vegas, Nevada.

You'll know you've "gone Hollywood" when you read about Universal City-Walk. You'll want music and a margarita when you read about Festival Plaza in Rosarito Beach, Mexico. And you'll feel you should change into your toga when you read about the Forum Shops at Caesars.

Mall competition may have gotten keener, but in response, mall developers and their creative teams of architects and designers are meeting that challenge by inventing new visual concepts. Being different is no longer something important; it's vital.

ARIZONA CENTER

Phoenix, Arizona

It's the spectacular rooftop design of Arizona Center that establishes the look and identity of this extraordinary shopping mall. Located adjacent to a busy urban office/hotel complex set within the desert landscape of Arizona, this folded plane rooftop which shades an enormous crescent building has become a recognizable symbol to area residents. Office tenants and hotel guests look down upon this dramatic "fan" architecture — providing an aesthetic view of what might have been an ordinary shopping center rooftop or parking lot!

This very strong graphic image is captured and recaptured throughout the environs of the mall. Dominating the stucco exterior of the mall is a translation of the crescent/fan image — fabricated with energy efficient light bulbs inside gilded, glass enclosures that are recessed into the stucco wall surface. The image glows as evening draws on.

With Phoenix being a desert community, an oasis-like garden landscape was designed as an integral part of the complex. Replaying the design theme, gardens of palm trees are set amidst lattice-canopied walkways (fan-shaped lattice, of course) gracefully inviting pedestrians to stroll the shaded walkways. The sights and sounds of water — cascading over stone or running like little rivers — add to the atmosphere of refreshment.

Demonstrating brilliantly how the design of an edifice can be carried forth to provide a shopping center with an integrated identity, the collaborating creative team at Arizona Center has restated the crescent image onto a crisp memorable logo. It appears consistently on all printed pieces, on shopping bags, on visual displays and signage. Such fidelity to single-mindedness of design has achieved high consumer recognition for Arizona Center.

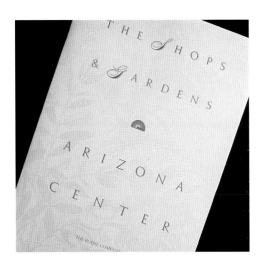

Architect: *Carol Shen, ELS/Elbansi & Logan Architects, Berkeley, CA*
Design Consultants and Environmental Graphics: *Communication Arts Inc., Boulder, CO*
Landscape Architect: *The SWA Group, Sausalito CA*
Photographer: *Greg Hursley*

Question: When is a shopping mall a year 'round fiesta? Answer: when it's the Bazaar del Mundo.

Situated in the very popular Old Town section of San Diego, the Bazaar itself has become a leading tourist destination — known not only for its extraordinarily colorful retail shops, but also for its community festivals, cultural exhibits and folkloric entertainment.

Color, color, color. That's the Bazaar's pervasive theme. The splashes of red, yellow, orange and magenta are as fiery as the flamenco dancing on weekend afternoons. The entryway, the kiosks, the lushly flowered garden courtyard and sparkling fountains, the restaurants, the stores themselves — all reflect California's rich Hispanic heritage.

What is particularly striking is that — unlike the mix of divergent store identities that is found at most shopping malls… at Bazaar del Mundo, there is only one "look". All the stores and restaurants carry forth the same colors, graphics and type faces. As you might expect with such consistency of image, the shopping bags, promotion pieces, mailers and catalog are also "absolute Bazaar"!

It is interesting to learn that this lively shopping mall is actually a restoration of a dilapidated motel which had seen its best days in the 1930's when it was built in authentic Mexican Colonial style. The underlying architecture (the inter-connected corridors and balconies) was meticulously restored by designer, Diane Powers, thereby creating Bazaar del Mundo's unique and unmistakable retail identity.

Owner, Designer and Restorer: *Diane Powers*
Original Architect: *Richard Requa*
Photographers: *Sandra Williams, Ted Walton*
Graphic Designer: *Deirdre Lee*

CLEARWATER MALL

Clearwater, Florida

Sometimes its the simplest elements that can contribute to a retail identity. Clearwater Mall took is first letter and its obvious visualization of "water" and created a logo that's a mammoth "C" with a rebus of waves and set it in a geometric triangle shape. Voila: instant recognition.

Customers see it from the highway, as they approach the mall and once they alight, they find it on collateral like the smartly designed shopping bag.

The atmosphere of the mall is a reflection of the uncluttered logo design. Neon is used everywhere, creating simple shapes like waves and sunbursts. Especially striking are the neon arches that form the "spine" of leaping dolphins.

Bright and clean and clear: Clearwater!

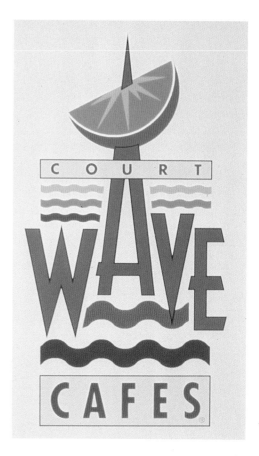

Design and Graphics: *SDI-HTI, Cincinnati, OH*

DADELAND MALL

Miami, Florida

We've all heard of Disneyland and Legoland. But what in the world is Dadeland? No, it's not a theme park, but the design team at one of South Florida's major shopping centers has created a mall that has much of that same theatrical environment.

Dadeland Mall is palm trees, palm trees, palm trees. Like snapping your fingers, the center's image comes to you in a flash. There are palm trees everywhere inside the mall — lining walkways, encircling sparkling fountains, reaching gracefully up to the ornate dome that marks the centerpoint of the mall.

To translate the palm tree theme into an identifiable graphic, a single palm leaf has been artfully photographed — the linear detail of the leaf's formation making the image both aesthetic and memorable. This graphic is used faithfully on all Dadeland Mall communiques: directories, calendars, mailing pieces and promotion collateral. Especially beautiful is the Dadeland Mall glossy

shopping bag. Sporting a bright yellow rope-handle that picks up the bright yellow of the Dadeland logo script, the bag has the extra added attraction of a superimposed high-fashion photo.

Dadeland Mall's impressive tropical theme has not only established a strong identity among Florida shoppers, it has also made an impact in helping the mall to market to the important travel and tourism industry. (Even their international marketing video is packaged in a palm tree logo box!)

In one beautiful shopping locale, Dadeland Mall has captured the flavor of Miami and the essence of a vacation paradise.

Architect: *Weed & Johnson*
Graphic Design: *Yamila Sanchez*
Photographer: *Scherley Busch*

DOWNTOWN PLAZA

Sacramento, California

The grand opening of the Downtown Plaza shopping mall was also a grand reaffirmation of California's capital city, Sacramento. The architecture and design of the shopping center is an imaginative translation of the famous capital dome. In addition, since a major citywide objective was the revitalization of the downtown urban scene, the mall has been energetically integrated into the city itself. Instead of closing the center and shutting it away from its environs, the designers have allowed the grid of the city to flow through, connecting the retail hub to the rest of the city. The new Downtown Plaza truly enjoys an intimate relationship with the historic spaces and places.

The most dominant visual component of the center's design is the dome/rotunda which is a stunning translation of the state capital's exquisite historical dome building.

It is this dome shape which also has set the tone for the geometric forms found throughout all the center's graphics and collateral. The curved shapes along with squares, zigzags and rectangles repeat themselves on directories, invitations, event calendars, brochures, etc. The result: a totally unified graphic story — clearly telegraphing one focused statement.

Besides the successful visual message conveyed by Downtown Plaza, the creative team also established an "audio" identity. Having purchased the rights to the song "Downtown", they adapted both music and lyrics for radio and television. Taking it still one step further, they employed the lyrics in headline copy and billboards. Nothing has been overlooked in this well-conceived program of retail image and graphic identity.

Architect: *The Jerde Partnership, Venice, CA*
Creative Design: *2M&G Marketing Arts, Tiburon, CA*
Photographer: *Tom Myers*
Developer: *The Hahn Company*

Architect and Contractor: *Marnell Corrao, Las Vegas, NV*
Interior Designers: *Dougall Design Associates, Inc., Los Angeles, CA*
Photographer: *Jeff Gale*

Main Street, Old Rome! Shoppers who visit Las Vegas soon find themselves transported back in time to an era of chariots, gladiators, philosophers and orators, Roman revelry and mythological gods. The spectacular architectural design of The Forum Shops at Caesars captures the grandiose "universe" in which the legendary emperor reigned. And this image and identity remain faithful in every facet of design and communications.

Storefronts and facades resemble an ancient Roman streetscape, with immense columns and arches, central piazzas, ornate fountains and classic statuary. Overhead, a "heavenly" painted, barrel-vaulted ceiling emulates the beauty of the Mediterranean sky.

Access to the Forum entrance (one steps right off the famous Las Vegas "strip" into this ancient world) makes a startling first impression with the brilliant Quadriga statue — four gold-leafed horses and charioteer, dramatically positioned high above the entryway.

The Fountain of the Gods, set in one of the piazzas under a massive domed rotunda, is sculpted with extra-ordinary authenticity — featuring a heroic Jupiter, a regal Neptune and the graceful winged Pegasus.

In another piazza, the Festival Fountain astounds customers with its seven minute fantasy sound and light spectacle. Lasers, lights, music, sound effects, audio animatronics, video projections, cascades of jewel-lit waters — all theatrically produced for the pleasure of the shoppers.

The Roman experience is sustained through the design of all collateral. Caesar's famous crown, the laurel wreath, is used as a dominant motif: on stationery, on baseball caps and T-shirts. The shopping bag is, not unexpectedly, coveted by shoppers: it features a scene of toga-ed citizens on a bustling Roman street.

Through its retail image and graphic identity, The Forum at Caesars has achieved a reputation as a most unique destination marketplace.

GALLERIA AT TYLER

Riverside, California

The design team refers to it as a "waggly wiggle waggle". And though it sounds frivolous, by no means is it so. The graphic identity for the Galleria at Tyler mall emerged as a very strategic gesture that was aimed at enhancing the fashion image of the center.

The graceful expressive zig-zag motif, coupled with the elegant custom-designed logotype convey a sense of style and flair. The first statement is made as shoppers approach the mall. The serpentine graphic commands

attention as it highlights tall, dramatic arched entryways.

That graphic identity is never far from the customer's eye. It is used extensively on directories and all informational signage. Nothing is overlooked: not custom carts, not even parking structure walls.

The visual continuity is maintained via Tyler mall's advertising, promotion and catalogs. Especially attractive are items like the shopping bags, shirts and hats, where the rhythm of the design is especially eye-catching and reinforces the memorability of the mall's very distinctive identity.

Architect: *Callison Partnership, San Diego, CA*
Graphics Design: *Communication Arts, Boulder, CO*
Advertising Design: *Wiley Designs*

SUPERSTITION SPRINGS CENTER

Mesa, Arizona

For city slickers who imagine that there's nothing but wild and rugged open spaces way out west in Arizona's Superstition Mountains, we have a secret surprise. At the foot of the mountains resides a most innovative new shopping center. Aptly titled Superstition Springs Center, the mall has been brilliantly designed to combine an up-to-date shopping arena with the environment of the desert.

The landscaping for the center was created by the Arizona Botanical Garden. Thus, instead of the usual shopping mall shrubbery, the customer experiences an authentic sense of space. There are two marked theme trails, a Play Canyon Playground, an amphitheater used for concerts and special events as well as giant bamboo groves that provide cool shade — seemingly miraculous when summer heat soars to 100-plus.

The architecture of the mall is "round" — providing a flow and expansiveness in harmony with the west's characteristically wide open spaces. The mall layout is round, walls of buildings are rounded and even the streetways are curved. The Superstition Springs logo is a strong, almost visibly vibrating "SS" — rendered with repeat curve lines that can't be missed on shopping bags and other collateral.

In addition to the logo graphic, the concept of outdoor desert photography is used collaboratively as a thematic element in establishing the Center's image. Ads, gift certificates and shopping bags are unmistakably recognizable.

Most remarkably, the graphics and terrestrial photography transcend the cliche, succeeding in conveying a smart, contemporary (and very memorable) retail identity.

Architect:
Architechtronics, Phoenix, AZ
Graphics Design:
Hershey Communications, Irvine, CA

The hot, lifeless air

suddenly cools.

The wind quickens.

The sky rumbles.

And all at once the

night becomes electric.

Something's out there.

You used to think there should be snow, but you came to realize that the holidays aren't a place, they're a feeling. A feeling you can only get by being there.

Something's out there.

SUPERSTITION SPRINGS CENTER

SUPERSTITION SPRINGS CENTER

Gift Certificate

SUPERSTITION SPRINGS CENTER

Gift Certificate

SUPERSTITION SPRINGS CENTER

Gift Certificate

Architectural Design/Environmental Design: *Karen Beckwith,*
Beckwith Barrow Ltd., Garrison, N.Y.
Project Director: *Jill Butler, GRID, USA, Paris, France*

The lovely town of Lille in France is known for its high fashion textile design, and as such, is the host city for the annual international textile trade fair.

It is understandable why — when challenged with the renovation of an outdated, dark and unfriendly mid-size shopping mall, the designers who were engaged to renovate Les Tanneurs decided to look to Lille's fashion/textile roots to create a fresh identity.

This section of the city was once a center for leather manufacturing and leather tanning. Part of the design concept was to make visual reference to that history and is conveyed by an engraved style mural depicting an antique leather tannery which runs along the soffit cut between floors around the escalators. In dramatic counterpoint to the antique mural, the use of bold, modern colors contemporizes the center, making it attractive for the city's new younger population.

The colors emerge, making their primary statement in the form of bright fabric banners, fashioned to mimic the look of hand-drawn textile fabrics (once again, expressing the historical theme.)

Interestingly, the mall features three different exterior facades — each with a different architectural rhythm. To bring the three facades into harmony and to differentiate them, a different color combination of textile banner designs begins at each entryway, and then — suspended from the mall's ceiling — each color group winds its way along one of three primary pathways. towards the center atrium, culminating in an unexpected crash of sculptural color.

The logotype for "Les Tanneurs" was created in the same hand-of-the-artist style of the textile designs, a reiteration of the mall's theme and identity.

UNIVERSAL CITYWALK

Universal City, California

Hurray for Hollywood! Where else could we find a retail image and identity that makes its statement from NOT having a single cohesive and integrated design?

Come and stroll Universal CityWalk. Step along a fantasy L.A. shopping boulevard that's mixed and matched to reflect the energy and diversity of this incomparable city. At this rambling outdoor shopping promenade, we see a range of startlingly different storefront designs — each jostling for attention. We see neon and comic book images, patchwork facades and monstrously scaled dimensional signs. A fervid buzz of different graphic identities.

But... it is this very assemblage of fanciful architectural gestures that does, ultimately,

provide a single strong retail image and identity. Altogether, this collage of colliding images coalesces to represent one common identity: this oh-so-L.A. shopping street of entertainment.

CityWalk is definitely an exception to most of the criteria for this book. The CityWalk logo is used very sparingly. You won't find it on shopping bags or signage — on matchbooks or employee outfits. The wide range of retail stores have each been designed by different firms. And, thus, understandably, the ultimate identity of CityWalk should be credited to the many designers whose separate creations have been combined so energetically.

If this seems to be a contradiction... I believe the reality is: that this unorthodox, fragmen-

tary hodgepodge of architecture and design earns CityWalk a standing ovation for achieving its retail image and identity through its attitude and personality.

Executive Architect: *Daniel, Mann, Johnson and Mendenhall, Los Angeles, CA*
Design Architect: *The Jerde Partnership, Los Angeles, CA*

UNIVERSITY MALL

Tampa, Florida

When a shopping center takes on a contemporary positioning with a tag line "Anything But Square"… what would you imagine the architects and designers would create? Obviously,— rounds, circles, curves. And clear, crisp pizzazzy primary colors.

Approaching the entrance to University Mall, you know immediately that this shopping center is "not square". The tall, illuminated cylindrical tower greets you, adorned with its bold, colorful moon logo. The free-spirited squiggle motifs used in the logo pop up everywhere as you enter the mall. They encircle the pillars of the mall corridors, they move around the circular ceiling trellis that is suspended below the natural light ceiling.

Meticulous detailing of chandeliers and light fixtures provide a luminous rhythm of moons and suns, serving to further enhance the

clean, fresh, contemporary environment. Perhaps the most charming translation of the squiggle motif is in the airy center court, where they segue into an aquatic theme. Neon "waves" swim beneath the skylight roof… along with schools of brightly colored fish.

Sun, moon, ocean, light, air. This sense of space and brightness is experienced by shoppers as they stroll throughout the curved pathways of the mall. The abstract flow of the elements of nature provide a distinctive environment for University Mall, making it one of Tampa's most visually pleasing and graphically identifiable shopping centers.

Architect: *Anthony Belluschi Architects, Ltd., Chicago, IL*
Environmental Graphics Designer: *SDI-HTI, Cincinnati, OH*
Photographers: *Aaron Kessler, George Cott/Croma, Inc.*

VALENCIA TOWN CENTER

Valencia, California

This charming retail shopping center draws its inspiration from the rich agricultural history of the surrounding Santa Clarita Valley. The project integrates references of early ranching with the Mission and Victorian influences indigenous to central California coastal communities.

The center's Mediterranean exterior is a collection of towers and sloped terra cotta tile roofs. Inside, a planned "urban main street" takes customers past a series of handsome murals depicting "The Orange Grove", "Our Valley", "Ranch Life" and "The People of the Valley" — each a proud representation of the lifestyles of the people who founded the territory.

A wonderful graphic that takes its cue from the flourishing orange groves is the orange crate label. It pops up, deliciously, everywhere: on shiny shopping bags, stationery and all promotion pieces. In addition, the orange crate label is interpreted on the exterior signage, food court signage and most dramatically on a huge, circular mosaic imbedded in the sidewalk at the main entryway to the mall.

One of the most entertaining and popular sites in the mall is the floor clock/time capsule. Patterned after early 20th century clocks, this timepiece's face is (of course) a great big Valencia orange. Encapsulated underneath it are a collection of historical objects which were contributed by area residents.

Towering palms and planters of abundant foliage, along with Spanish tile marble continue the staging of this lush, valley environment which successfully represents its historical past and unique identity.

Architecture & Environmental Graphics: *RTKL, Baltimore, Maryland*
Paul Jacob, AIA, Project Director
Phil Engelke and Ann Dudrow, Graphic Designers
Photographers: *David Whitcomb, Paul Bielenberg*

Valencia Town Center is a development of The Newhall
Land and Farming Company in partnership with Urban
Shopping Centers, Inc.

THE PLAZA AT WEST COVINA

West Covina, California

Everybody's talking about those "little critters". Those imaginatively designed and fabricated bent metal sculptures that have helped endow the Plaza at West Covina with high recognition in the competitive Greater Los Angeles area.

Ranging in size from 18 inches to several feet long, the whimsical interpretations of birds, cows, mice, and dragonflys decorate the mall — on fountains, on sconces — everywhere. Even after shoppers depart from the parking lot, it is likely that a critter or two is riding along; these folk-inspired art images reappear on promotion brochures, calendars, directories, as well as on T-shirts, mugs and styrofoam cups from take-out cafes.

The concept of folk-like art from local history provided the perspective for the design team's plan to establish West

Covina as "different". Like "the critters", nature motifs reflecting the area's history were created. A walnut leaf, an oak leaf and acorns, the sun and a spiral graphic derived from the art of the original native basket weavers are fabricated of the same bent metal.

The decision to emphasize the use of metal as a "theme material" was a conscious decision to enhance the unity of the mall's design. Like "the critters" and the nature images, the pole-mounted illuminated banners that border the mall's periphery are fabricated of sculpted aluminum, using the same bright colors found inside the center. At day's end, they form welcoming beacons for consumers in the area creating an identity that is as recognizable at night as during the day.

Architect:
Paul Jacob, AIA, RTKL Associates Inc., Los Angeles, CA
Graphics:
Ann Dudrow, Charlie Greenawalt, RTKL Associates Inc., Baltimore, MD
Photographer:
David Whitcomb

FESTIVAL PLAZA

Rosarito, Baja California

More than a center for shopping, more than a crossroads of eateries and nightclubs, more than a glitzy eight-story hotel, the new Festival Plaza is a never-to-be-forgotten playground for grownups.

Imagery, colors, strobing lights and graphics that move — all, relentlessly convey a carnival atmosphere. Located a half hour south of San Diego, Festival Plaza is pure "border architecture" — a taste of tawdry translated with witty sophistication and bursting upon the scene like a Mexican mardi gras.

With its landmark rollercoaster facade (60 feet high) and its crowd-pleasing techno-wonders such as a suspension bridge and a Ferris wheel, the Plaza establishes itself as the first major new tourist attraction for Rosarito Beach in some 70 years.

Consumers find two-and-a-half acres in which to revel. They encounter lifesize figures and statues, planted casually and surprisingly throughout — like a splendid cartoon-y cow and an enormous serpent mascot which seems to emerge from the ground as it coils around the Plaza's sound booth.

Flamboyant and fanciful, the colors and imagery of Festival Plaza continue to beguile customers on vibrant signage, riotously-colored banners, bags, menus, brochures, invitations and bumper stickers.

If quirky, zany Festival Plaza seems to scream for applause, it surely earns its bows — having created an energetic retail identity all its own.

EL FESTIVAL

A Celebration of Life & Culture

You are exclusively invited to join us for :

EL FESTIVAL

The Grand Opening of:

FESTIVAL Plaza®

A Celebration of Life & Culture

Saturday, July 30th in Rosarito Beach Mexico.

Festivities will include:

VIP Reception: 6pm to 8pm in the hotel lobby area.

Dedication of the Plaza: 8pm in the Plaza and amphitheatre area.

Scheduled performer: Michael McDonald 9pm in the amphitheatre.

Fireworks Extravaganza: Approximately 11pm.

Complimentary cocktails and a buffet will be served before and after the concert.

Admission to other venues.

R.S.V.P.

FRIDAY & SATURDAY

FESTIVAL PLAZA INVITES YOU:

FESTIVAL MEXICANO

A Celebration of Life & Culture

ROSARITO BAJA CALIFORNIA

FESTIVAL Plaza®

FESTIVAL Plaza®

Design Team: *Team Alix*
Guillermo Martinez de Castro, Principal in Charge
Luis Guillermo Pereira Lozada, Project Architect
Juan Manuel Yi Echauri, Art Director
Landscape Architect: *Andy Spurlick, Marty Poirier*
Interiors: *Sam Hatch, Hatch Design, Costa Mesa, CA*
Photographer: *Rick Goddard, Action Photography, Laguna Hills, CA*

PHIPPS PLAZA

Atlanta, Georgia

The gracious architectural renovation of Phipps Plaza has prompted many to call it the "Jewel of the South." It has achieved a reputable identity of its own — having been designed to mirror the interior of a grand Southern hotel or mansion.

In contrast to many of today's contemporary and sometimes glitzy hi-tech malls, Phipps Plaza takes a completely traditional approach. Rather than endure the environment of long walkways and corridors, shoppers are meant to feel as though they are passing through the rooms of an elegant mansion. Memories of Tara are evoked. Stately columns are a commanding sight in the large court areas. Everywhere — from ceiling to floor, the details are meticulous. There are eleven variations of imported marble and granite. At the center of the Monarch Court, the enormous elliptical skylight accentuates the recently added third shopping level.

Most elegant of all is the dramatic grand staircase in the Court of the South. It is actually a grand double staircase similar to those found in the mansions of yesteryear. Above it, the hand-painted ceiling serves to enhance the magnificent showpiece chandelier.

The Southern theme is carried throughout by many marvelous design details. Marble flooring medallions depict flowers of the South — magnolias, camellias, dogwoods. This flower theme continues throughout the mall — picked up as accent motifs on railings, upholstery and light fixtures. Exclusive Phipps Plaza notecards were created — carrying the magnolia image. Shopping bags, press kits, directories and souvenir mugs replay the Phipps Plaza gold script logo on the rich green marble-textured background. With all this attention to detail, it comes as no surprise that Phipps Plaza has earned more than a dozen awards of distinction.

Architect: *Thompson, Ventulett, Stainback & Associates, Inc., Architects, Atlanta, GA*
Photographer: *Brian Gassel, TVS & A*

88

FOOD GLORIOUS FOOD

If dining is one of your passions…
we suggest you make a list of the
restaurants in this chapter. Each is a
total and spectacular visual experience.
And if your travels take you to the
indicated city, we implore you to have
a "look see".

What wonders have been wrought
with the simple wedge shape that now
pervades Wolfgang Puck's Cafes. And,
as long as we're name-dropping, if you
could visit Red Sage in Washington,
D.C., you'd understand, in an instant,
why it's popular with Bill and Hillary.

If theater or business take you to the
Century City area of LA, it's almost
impossible to miss the mammoth hull
of DIVE's yellow submarine. It's a
make-believe underwater adventure
— something you might expect if
Steven Spielberg was involved (and
guess what: he is!)

Yes, this chapter includes the new and
the outrageous. But it also pays
respect to places that have maintained
the magic of their identity, though
years have passed. Where is it Christmas every day of the year, but at the
Russian Tea Room? And could
anything be more quintessentially
"New York, New York" than the
Rainbow Room?

The various design teams involved in
each of these restaurant projects have
earned high praise for their creativity
and ingenuity. But more than that,
they have shown their commitment to
translating essence into reality:
bringing a restaurant's character to
life by dedication to design and detail.

RED SAGE

Washington, D.C.

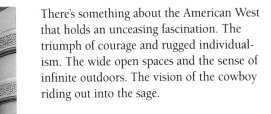

There's something about the American West that holds an unceasing fascination. The triumph of courage and rugged individualism. The wide open spaces and the sense of infinite outdoors. The vision of the cowboy riding out into the sage.

Red Sage has captured and imprinted the visual images of the American frontier —

achieving success as one of Washington's most popular, most recognized restaurants. The designers chose the artifacts and symbols of the West — everything from tools to decorations as their primary inspiration source.

The imposing steerhead logo is rendered in a rough-hewn, technique — a style that continues consistently through all graphic presentation and into the design of the restaurant itself. The environment of Red Sage sets the mood for the dining experience as soon as a customer steps inside: dark wood, timbered and tin ceilings, a stone and forged iron stairway, the voluptuous hearth, red leather booths, buffalo and cowhide upholstery, bison chandeliers, antler wall fixtures, a custom-woven bandana carpet and an extraordinary "Fire, Air and Water" mural.

The restaurant is a showcase of art and craftsmanship. But as it is a visual feast, so, too does it successfully enhance Mark Miller's "modern Western cuisine". Meals are served on Red Sage's exclusive dinnerware designed to compliment the logo and graphics. Even the table tops and bar tops have been specially crafted of custom-dyed concrete with barbed wire insets.

The strong graphic motifs and lively colors make their way brilliantly onto every printed piece — from menus to wine bottle labels. This combination of visual and culinary artistry makes a dazzling statement — explaining whimsically: how the West has been won again!

Architecture and Interior Design: *Stephen Samuelson, Harry Daple, Studio Arquitectura, Santa Fe, NM*
Graphic Design: *Hasten Design Studio, Inc., Washington, DC*
Photographers: *Ron Solomon, Baltimore, MD ©1992*
Stuart Diekmeyer, Washington, DC

COYOTE CAFE

Santa Fe, New Mexico

One visit to Santa Fe, New Mexico and a first-time visitor is captivated by the breathtaking beauty of the landscape and realizes how the natural light and shadows inspired such great artists as Georgia O'Keeffe. It's a land of sensitivity, of spirituality — complete with a culture of folkways and folk stories.

Surely the tales of the howling coyote were the inspiration for the renowned Coyote Cafe. Matchbooks with the cunning coyote silhouette can be found on living room coffee tables from San Francisco to New York, from Chicago to Boston. This is a retail identity that has achieved a national reputation.

It begins within the environs of the restaurant itself — a mixture of traditional Santa Fe architecture with a playful take on the region's cultural heritage. Indian and Mexican motifs are used throughout. Dancing skeletons are inspired by Mexican All Soul's Day and an Indian pattern is painted on the adobe walls. The color theme is bright turquoise, gold and red — employed as as a tile pattern in the open kitchen… and again repeated on the serving ware. (Food presentation is a priority since Coyote Cafe's unique contemporization of southwestern cuisine is what attracts its loyal following.)

On a ledge above the bar, whimsical folk-art wooden animals (howling coyotes among them) look down on the crowds of diners. The angular wrought-iron dining chairs are upholstered with animal skins.

With appetite satiated, customers may leave the restaurant … but the howling coyote follows them. First to the retail store in the building where an abundance of Coyote Cafe hot sauces and seasonings, packaged foods, coffees and teas and cookbooks are for sale. And then there's the Coyote Cafe catalog — cucina by mail! Unabashedly, this trailblazing restaurant has achieved an identity as the quintessential contemporary southwestern.

Architecture and Interior Design: *Stephen Samuelson, Harry Daple, Studio Arquitectura, Santa Fe, NM*
Graphic Book and Catalog Design: *Fifth Street Design, Berkeley, CA*
Photographers: *Larry Horton, Corrales, NM; Santagto, Santa Fe, NM*

Theatricality! In design, in atmosphere, in presentation… this is the essence of the identity of the Rainbow Room as it glimmers and shimmers 65 stories above the heart of New York City — all aglow in its glamorous $20 million renovation.

Capturing remembrances of things past… yet, at the same time, striking a balance between old and new was the challenge for both architect and graphic designer.

Nostalgia, of course, played a key role in re-interpreting this legendary night spot. But, how to express it in a contemporary idiom? Architect and graphic designer collaborated and conceived the Rainbow Room complex as a kind of a stage set — everything from the decor to

the staff uniforms to the service plates at the tables was designed to come together to make a coherent whole.

From the moment the elevator doors part at the Rainbow Room lobby, the image begins. A colonnade of lighted glass columns bid welcome. The geometric play of verticals, horizontals and diagonals dominate everywhere. The curve of the streamlined mahogany bar. The patterns in carpeting and fabrics.

In fact, the geometric theme becomes an actual "experience" as you move into the "Room" itself: you enter the dramatic space from corners, on the diagonal, and down a few steps. Beneath the ceiling's majestic dome, the original

compass pattern of wood inlay in the center of the revolving dance floor has been meticulously restored.

At the table, the stunning service platter makes its geometric statement with the brilliant "Rainbow" logo design. It is a graphic that is faithfully recreated on all brochures, menus, stationery, invitations and collateral.

Call it "American Modernism"… call it "swank"… in both character and identity, the Rainbow Room is an impressive collaboration of all the disciplines of design.

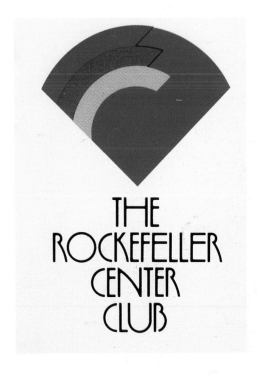

THE
ROCKEFELLER
CENTER
CLUB

The Pleasure of Doing Business
The Rockefeller Center Club

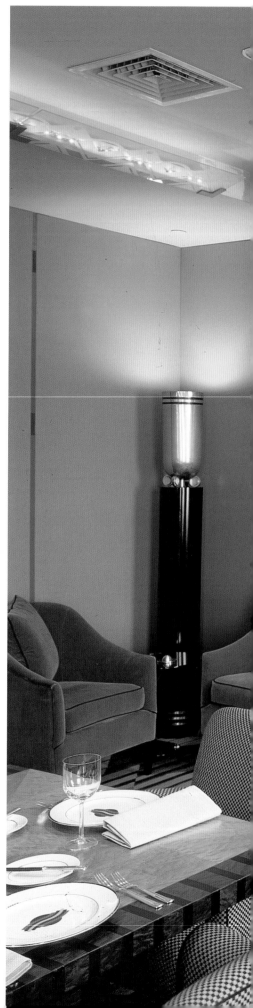

Architect: *Hardy Holzman Pfieffer Associates, New York, NY*
Graphic Designer: *Milton Glaser, Inc., New York, NY*
Photographers: *Christopher Little, Frederick Charles*

RED TOMATO

Chicago, Illinois

"Red Tomato" is not only the name of this funky yet refined restaurant, it is also the main graphic course! The mosaic facade of fat red tomatoes, (which runs the full 48 feet of the front of the restaurant) telegraphs the identity in an instant. As a further clarification, high above the inviting peek-inside window one notices the friendly neon logo. The logo, which has a hand-lettered quality, conveys the comfortable, homey atmosphere of the restaurant itself.

With the mutual conviction that design should translate integrally via both their disciplines, the architect and the designer guided the logo and the tomatoes into every aspect of this project. The tomato symbol appears on a frosted glass panel in the vestibule which screens the seated customers from those just arriving. Then, bursting as a garden at harvest, the tomatoes and logo reappear on everything from menus to take-out bags, from flyers and T-shirts to pizza boxes. As part of the opening promotion for Red Tomato, a glossy black box containing a big, ripe beefsteak tomato was sent to restaurant critics and concierges around the city.

The place, the product, the identity, the image: inseparable! Interestingly, to give the hardworking tomato a break, a second

graphic was added — a stylized Art Deco image of a long-tressed woman who juggles tomatoes on the menu cover and flies across the catering menu and wine list. She adds flair and fun — enhancing the friendly humor of the Red Tomato's atmosphere.

The Red Tomato has become so well established by virtue of its visual identity that, despite its inauspicious location beneath the El in one of Chicago's districts-in-transition, it has become a destination restaurant.

WHERE FOOD

AND FUN

BECOME ONE

Architect: *Aumiller Youngquist, P.C., Chicago, IL*
Graphic Design: *JOED Design, Inc., Elmhurst, IL*
Photographer: *Mark Ballogg: Steinkamp/Ballogg, Chicago, IL*

RIKKI RIKKI

Kirkland, Washington

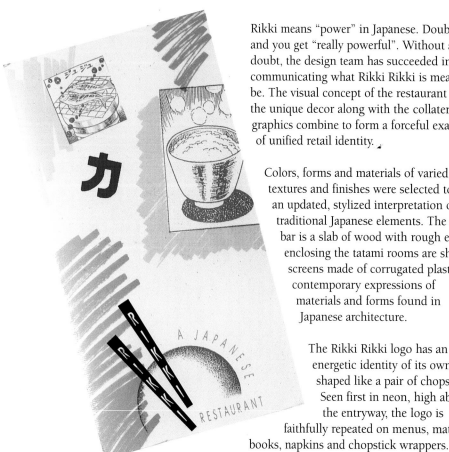

Rikki means "power" in Japanese. Double it and you get "really powerful". Without a doubt, the design team has succeeded in communicating what Rikki Rikki is meant to be. The visual concept of the restaurant and the unique decor along with the collateral graphics combine to form a forceful example of unified retail identity.

Colors, forms and materials of varied textures and finishes were selected to give an updated, stylized interpretation of traditional Japanese elements. The sushi bar is a slab of wood with rough edges; enclosing the tatami rooms are shoji screens made of corrugated plastic — contemporary expressions of materials and forms found in Japanese architecture.

The Rikki Rikki logo has an energetic identity of its own: it is shaped like a pair of chopsticks. Seen first in neon, high above the entryway, the logo is faithfully repeated on menus, matchbooks, napkins and chopstick wrappers.

Working as a counter graphic to the rigid angle chopstick motif is a graphic arc — resembling the shape of a fan. It, too, is repeated in neon and again, on the collateral. The shape is also carried through by the restaurant's furnishings: curved-back chairs and fan-shaped lighting fixtures.

Probably the most dominant graphic motif is the use of "manga" — a popular form of Japanese comic book entertainment. Giant wall murals display wild sketches of comic strip characters along with other abstract images such as postmarks from Tokyo and rice cooker instructions. Many of the whimsical graphic elements have also been captured (along with the Rikki Rikki logo) on the menu covers.

The result of Rikki Rikki's collaborative design efforts is a restaurant with a distinctive personality — one that measurably impacts customer recognition and customer loyalty.

Architect/Interior Designer: *Mesher Shing & Associates, Seattle, WA*
Graphic Design: *Hornall Anderson Design Works, Seattle, WA*
Photographer: *Dick Busher*

Mother to the Chinese was a woman 女 with her breasts drawn in. They pictured her first as 安 then as 安 to give her balance 夏. The final form of this character is 母. Used by itself it is generally pronounced (with the addition of several kana which indicate respect) OKĀSAN. This is the most popular Japanese word for mother, but to be understood it must be pronounced with a distinctly long Ā—OKĀSAN—to distinguish it from OKASAN

RUSSIAN TEA ROOM

New York, New York

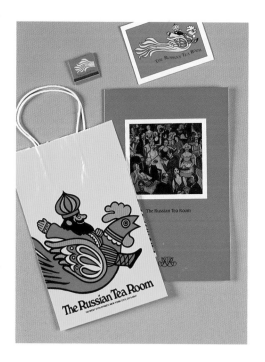

Here, at this world-famous restaurant, we find the epitome of design that is regarded by some as "gilding the lily". Everywhere — bright colors with a decor that gleams, glistens and tinkles. The atmosphere of the Russian Tea Room envelopes you and embraces you. It's an exhilarating environment of festivity and entertainment — the mood of Christmas all year long. There are few more festive places for one to celebrate a special occasion.

To customers who return to the Russian Tea Room after any lengthy absence, "the place never changes". That, of course, is the strength of the consistency of image and identity — magnificently retained despite the various and subtle changes that have, in actuality, occurred over the restaurant's history.

Art deco reigns. With details and ornaments, mirrors and brass trims, and eclectic paintings everywhere — each one different but all of them celebrating the art of life! Green and red dominate — but especially red. Owner Faith Stewart-Gordon likes to explain how red, in Russian (kras.ny), means "life". . . and how the root of that word is the same as that for "beauty" (kras.ivu).

Two graphic motifs emerge as recognizable identities: the ornate script of "RTR" and the whimsical mascot "Ivan the Lovable" who flies atop his bird on matchbooks and menus.

There is much that customers can take with them from the Russian Tea Room beside romantic memories. Now, there is logo merchandise, like the "Ivan the Lovable" sweatshirt and the bright yellow carry bags. And even more exciting, the Russian Tea Room cookbook — secret recipes that carry the taste of RTR into the kitchens of customers — however far away their homes might be. Nas darovya!

Design Concept: *Faith Stewart-Gordon, Owner*
Photographer: *Jerry and Robert Ruotolo*

DIVE!

Los Angeles, California

America's classic submarine sandwich has been reinvented and thrust into a spotlight of its own with the opening of DIVE! restaurant. There's not a moment's doubt as to the main menu — from the first encounter with the exterior (a gigantic life-size 30-foot yellow nose cone of a whimsical submarine) to the experience of entering the "hatch" door of the interior of the hull-shaped environment.

Both aesthetically and technically, customers take a dive — stepping aboard an imaginary, tongue-in-cheek submarine, complete with metal girder construction, portholes, a working periscope and "torpedo" barstools. Inspired by the fanciful mind of co-owner Steven Spielberg, a sophisticated multi-sensory presentation takes customers on a virtual underwater voyage — experiencing the sounds and sights of uncharted waters from around the world.

Everything is integrated into the submarine concept — from the tablescape on which the food is served to the bathrooms with their yellow and black safety-striping doors. Menus and an enormous range of printed collateral materials reinforce the identity. The waitpersons become "crew" garbed in their specially designed DIVE! uniforms.

For customers, an extensive range of DIVE! logo merchandise has been created: watches, workshirts, sweatshirts, T-shirts, boxer shorts, dog tags, key chains, baseball caps, bomber and leather jackets.

Not one detail has been overlooked in presenting a single, unified message for DIVE! via both merchandising and marketing — identifying the restaurant clearly for what it serves, what it is and how it wants to be recognized.

Project Concept/Design/Managing Partner: *The Levy Restaurants, Chicago, IL*
Architect/Interior Design: *Joe Meisel, Meisel Associates, Limited, Chicago, IL*
Graphic Design and Product Design: *Adrienne Weiss Corporation, Chicago, IL*

ZUNI GRILL

Irvine, California

In deference to the American Indian tribe of its namesake, Zuni Grill, a cozy upscale eatery has created an environment that simulates an ancient native cave dwelling.

Faux-granite blocks topped with onyx-like panels serve as an entry to the restaurant. Further enhancing the primal design, raw colored concrete sweeps through the space at the floor level, only to be stopped by large broken fragments of flagstone. Hand-weathered and painted wall surfaces of sunset hues cast a warm glow. Protruding beams of burnished metal layered across the space serve as a rough ceiling.

Furnishings are also "native". Heavy woven fabric, reminiscent of Indian blankets are used on the seating. Lighting is "cave-like" — soft and dim. Here and there, brightly colored abstract art adds a spirited accent and helps provide the contrasting contemporary attitude.

The cave wall architecture establishes the graphic theme for the menus, matchbooks, stationery and all other collateral. Backgrounds mimic the rough stone texture with random renderings of Indian pictographs. The Zuni Grill logo has a marvelous mystery about it. A hand-lettered design, it appears like a word scratched out on a primitive cave painting.

The beauty of Zuni's design and embellishments achieves, without a doubt, a sophisticated yet primitive image. But there are those who would say that Zuni's identity is more in its "spirit."

Interior Design: *Hatch Design Group*
Costa Mesa, CA
Graphics: *On the Edge, Newport Beach, CA*
Photographer: *Don Romero*

WOLFGANG PUCK CAFES

Los Angeles, California

What wonders Barbara Lazaroff has worked with the shape of a wedge of pizza. Here, at the Wolfgang Puck Cafes, one not only smells the aroma of… and enjoys the flavor of Wolfgang's now-famous pies… but one "sees" the pizza — everywhere.

The entranceway, the wall facings, the pizza oven — all are designed as glistening mosaics, featuring colorful ceramic wedge-shaped pieces. Even tables and chairs have been meticulously designed to maintain the integrity of the creative design theme. The formica tabletops are dotted with colored triangles and the chairbacks are actually shaped like pizza wedges and painted in the same bright colors seen everywhere. Attention has been paid to locations at which patios have been added for outdoor dining: flower pots and umbrellas continue the theme with patterns of colorful wedges.

Floors, ceilings, light fixtures — all are theatrically created to reflect and reinforce the essence of the Wolfgang Puck Cafes. As you would expect, menus, napkins, business cards spotlight the pizza-pie logo. The bakers wear T-shirts and caps with the company logo. (All of which are available for dedicated diners to purchase.) Waiters and waitresses also carry the theme via their attire: each wears a crisp white logo-ed apron over a long-sleeved shirt in one of the colors from the sizzling palette.

(Editor's Note: If the design and the product in this case seem like a perfect marriage, readers may enjoy noting that Wolfgang Puck and Barbara Lazaroff are husband and wife!)

Restaurateur, Architectural Designer and Co-Owner of Wolfgang Puck Cafes:
Barbara Lazaroff, A.S.I.D., Imaginings Interior Design, Inc., Beverly Hills, CA

THE GOOD DINER

New York, New York

Like all things that fall out of fashion, there is a time when a good idea reemerges with a new gusto. So it has been with diners. They have returned… each of them with a new kind of flair that signals the "in" places to dine.

But there is only one diner that has earned its way to heaven. And that is The Good Diner located at (of all places) 42nd Street in Manhattan). Talk about retail identity… the graphic symbol for this diner is a coffee cup that has been elevated to sainthood! The lit-up halo blesses everything in sight.

It is truly a divine graphic program, with this artful identity rendered on menus, announcements, matchbooks, signage and stationery.

Passers-by can't help being attracted by The Good Diner's bright awning and outdoor signage. Stepping inside, the wonderful interior more than fulfills their expectations. Stools and banquettes are upholstered in bright primary colors and floors and tabletops are covered with three types of linoleum. Displayed on the walls are huge framed photocopies of archetypical diner objects, such as salt shakers and teabags. A series of 12 slightly different clocks hang over the counter — a throwback to the diner days when people really wolfed down their blue plate specials.

(I am obligated to mention that, one other factor responsible for The Good Diner's popularity, along with its heavenly retro design image… is its down to earth prices!)

Architect, Interior & Graphic Design:
Pentagram, New York, NY

116

CORONADO CAFES

Albuquerque, New Mexico

Lizards and eagles and snakes… oh my! Lizards and eagles and snakes… oh my! If Dorothy along with Toto and her entourage had to trek through this area to get to the Land of Oz, they would have found it more fun than fearsome. These wonderfully whimsical representations of Arizona wildlife make the food court at Coronado Center a real attraction for shoppers.

Elaborate in both design and fabrication, the lizards, eagles and snakes are just the starting points for establishing the Coronado Cafes' unique personality. Desert sunlight is seemingly invented, despite the location in the mall's lower level; a highly-theatrical ceiling treatment combines architecture and environmental graphics in a "symbolic" skylight which provides the illusion of outdoor brightness.

The idea of "fun" graphics pervades all aspects of this spacious mall dining site. Table tops are pinto-pony-patterned. A huge red chili pepper, rendered in neon, forms the Coronado Cafes logo. And that same graphic reappears in a number of locations and on a variety of collateral — reiterating the identity of this inviting, appetizing Southwestern-styled food court.

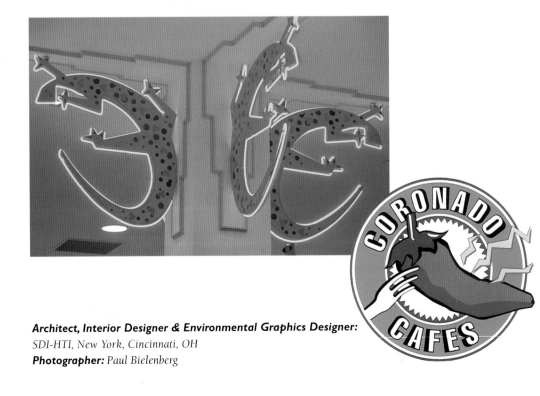

Architect, Interior Designer & Environmental Graphics Designer:
SDI-HTI, New York, Cincinnati, OH
Photographer: *Paul Bielenberg*

Celebrating the tradition of the American state fair, this design team has created a food court that fancifully plays off one of the heartland's most popular annual events. A nearly perfect pun, the name State Fare Food Court sets the stage for a wonderfully whimsical eating adventure.

Colors, shapes, flashing marquee lights, strobing neon, striped canvas awnings, illuminated arcades and amusement areas — all combine to convey the ambiance of the midway. Hurried diners may want to "eat and run" — but it's impossible to resist lingering in this very kinetic space which is designed with so many visual surprises. Larger-than-life iconographic images of the state fair meet customers at every turn; there's a towering cob of corn, an ice cream cone, a circus peanut and a hot dog. (And, oh yes, each of them serves to function as well as to decorate: this Lilliputian land of food sculptures covers structural columns and hides pipes!)

High above the food court, lights chase around a ferris wheel — suspended horizontally from the ceiling. There's also a pinwheel chandelier. Table tops feature nostalgic photos. And most fun of all are the farm-animal-chairs, seated at a counter that runs around the perimeter of the court's center — looking out and down to the shopping atrium below.

Graphically speaking, State Fare Food Court doesn't really devise a specific symbol from which to create signage. In fact, it is the architecture, itself, that is the signage! The inherent design theme and all its manifestations successfully create an identity which is cohesive and complete. Everything is harmoniously tied together — conveying the spirit and magic of a Minnesota state fair — albeit its location within the controlled dignity of the upscale Gaviidae Common retail center.

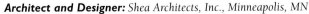

Architect and Designer: *Shea Architects, Inc., Minneapolis, MN*
Sculptor: *Dan Mackerman*
Photographer: *Christian Korab*

CALIFORNIA PIZZA KITCHEN

Los Angeles, California

The palm tree, the attractive open kitchen all tiled in shiny white, yellow and black along with the glorified aroma of cheeses, onion, garlic, chicken and other imaginative ingredients. It must be a California Pizza Kitchen!

This wonderful creative formula has succeeded in making CPK (they like that moniker, too) recognizable and welcome as the chain opens restaurants across the USA.

What better choice of a California icon than a palm tree? And the logo designer rendered it with ultra simplicity: in black silhouette on a grid that is reminiscent of the kitchen tiles that dominate the interior design of all CPK's.

The tri-color theme plays a most important part in the visual image: the white, yellow and black turns up everywhere — on all marketing and promotional material, on napkins, menus and placemats. There's a complete range of logo merchandise: hats, water bottles, golf accessories. Even the waitpersons "look" the part— crisply dressed in their black CPK aprons tied over their white shirts and yellow ties.

When a CPK opens in your town… you'll know it right away!

Graphic Design: *Rod Dyer, Rod Dyer Group,Inc., Los Angeles, CA*
Photographers: *Mark Ballogg: Steinkamp/Bellogg, Chicago, IL*
Hart Productions

APPLE COMPUTER CAFES

Off the Wall Cafe, Mega-Byte Cafe, Tech Talk Cafe
Cupertino, California

When is a company cafeteria not a company cafeteria? When the company is Apple Computer and when creative designers are engaged to transform the boring corporate food halls into chic eateries for hi-tech professionals.

Off the Wall Cafe, Mega-Byte Cafe and Tech Talk Cafe are three different retail locations — three food service locations, each in a different building at Apple Computer's Cupertino headquarters.

Each cafe has a distinctive art treatment — somewhat different but yet the same. The graphic IDs are individualized but all three design "packages" run parallel in concept: creating a trendy, hi-tech dining environment — attractive enough and with sufficient ambiance to entice computer professionals to remain on premises, rather than driving off to the local fast food or chain eateries for lunch or snacks.

Obviously, the creation of the three names was, itself, an important part of providing a personality for the in-house cafes. Aiming at giving employees a sense of ownership in their own dining spots, it was important that the titles reflect the idiom of the "techies".

From the nucleus of each cafe name came the creation of logo and graphic identity. And while there is a distinctiveness in each of the three cafes, there is also a "family resemblance" which was accomplished by use of computer-generated art.

If we follow Apple's logic, and recognize that they viewed the quality of their company's dining facilities as a visible benefit for employees, we might well acknowledge that retail-style identities are sure to become more and more common in corporate food environments.

Design Firm: *Profile Design/San Francisco, CA*
Art Director: *Thomas McNulty*
Fabricators: *Alan Wolf/California Model and Design*
Tony Erpelding/Erpelding Design
Off the Wall Cafe Designers: *Brian Jacobson and Thomas McNulty*
Mega-Byte Cafe Designer: *Thomas McNulty*
Tech Talk Cafe Designers: *Thomas McNulty and Jeanne Namkung*

COFFEE, COFFEE EVERYWHERE

The coffee bar boom is everywhere. Those addicted by espresso or impassioned by cappuccino can now get their fix from Seattle to Soho. (A New York Magazine article on "coffee talk" counts over 100 coffee bars in Manhattan alone!)

With the proliferation of coffee retailers and, as brand-name chains expand across the country, the challenge to attract a dedicated customer increases. Graphic image and identity become a vital ingredient in converting a customer from coffee-lover to coffee-loyalist.

Granted, the quality of the beans, the roasting, the coffee selections, gourmet accoutrements (and the service) can impact how consumers vote. However, all things being equal, picking a coffee star out of the coffee bar galaxy is surely affected by the image that is conveyed.

In this chapter, we take you coffee-bar hopping — spotlighting some of those retailers who have maximized their design identity through store presentation as well as collaborative environmental graphics.

STARBUCKS COFFEE COMPANY

Seattle, Washington

Why is it that when Starbucks opens a cafe in a new city, their arrival seems to be welcomed with an air of familiarity? True, they serve wonderful coffee. But, more than that, they've created a clearly recognizable identity. Store facades and store interiors — despite variations necessitated by physical location — are unmistakably Starbucks. The Starbucks striking siren logo and the company's distinctive green color quickly capture the attention of passers-by.

Stepping inside a Starbucks cafe, customers "experience" the coffee — enveloped by both the aroma and the environment. Starbucks coffee bags are displayed everywhere, becoming an integral part of the interior decor. The unique design of the bags reflects the richness of the product. Employing a

Store Design: *Brooke McCurdy, Starbucks Coffee Store Planning Department*
Graphic Design: *Hornall Anderson Design Works*
Photographers: *Tom McMackin, Bobo Alexander*

palette of warm tones of brown and red along with a graceful steam pattern, the packages make a powerful aesthetic statement about the quality and integrity of the product.

Variations of the steam pattern and the Starbucks icon find their way onto any and all items that customers see, touch or taste — from gift packs and shopping bags to the packaging for Starbucks' ever-growing line of coffee flavorings, granolas, etc. Of course, as one would expect, there are Starbucks logo coffee cups (both paper and ceramic), commuter mugs as well as coffee grinders and stoneware jars. The catalog, the servers' aprons and the comprehensive range of promotion pieces continue to capture and communicate the Starbucks story.

Interestingly, the expanding line of Starbucks products sometimes necessitates variations in type style, coloration or material. But because the commitment to the core design image is so successfully monitored, even where there are differences in visual or textural specifics, everything speaks the same language.

SEATTLE COFFEE ROASTERS

New York, New York

New York chic is what Seattle Coffee Roasters' image is all about! The name is enough to convey the coffee bar authenticity that has come to be associated with Seattle over these past few years. And wonderful sepia-tone historic photographs on the interior walls assure that the roots are real.

But, beyond that, this cafe's graphic identity is sleek and stylish. After all, it is located on lower Fifth Avenue in the shadow of New York's historic Flatiron Building. It caters to the advertising and fashion community that has recently moved to the neighborhood, en masse.

Black and gunmetal grey are sharp-edged against the stark off-white walls. Hard, industrial materials emphasize the contemporary environment. 17-foot high cast iron columns line the wall opposite the granite and metal serving counter.

The attitude of creative tension in the interior design is faithfully translated onto the logo: a hard-edged triangle with stylized type bordering each of the three sides. It makes an inviting statement on the store window. And, it is incorporated, with consistency, on all collateral— from stationery and menus to T-shirts, from mugs to ground-roast bags and pastry bags.

Seattle Coffee Roasters has defined itself to appeal to a very targeted audience, creating an identity that is as fashionable and trendy as the area in which it is located.

Architect/Graphic Design: Adams Rosenberg Kolb Architects, New York, NY
Photographer: Eduard Heuber, Arch Photo

CASABLANCA COFFEES

Chicago, Illinois

"Here's looking at you kid." Talk about instant identification, you don't need much more than a graphic rendering of this famous movie phrase to know the name of this coffee cafe has to be "Casablanca."

However, the designers of Casablanca Coffees preferred not to be parsimonious about their creative efforts in designing the integrated "package" for this Chicago retailer. They went the proverbial whole nine yards! Store planning and design, logotype, packaging, store signage and print collateral — all were developed around one core theme.

Graphics and architecture make a subtle reference to the movie "Casablanca", cleverly combining Art Deco details with the Moroccan influences represented in the film's location. The grey and white striped "tented" ceiling design is adapted as part of the packaging design and featured on everything from

coffee bean bags to gift boxes. The Casablanca typeface has a hint of Hollywood… and the interesting art detail above it was borrowed from a piece of Moroccan metalwork.

Even the names of the shop's quality roast blends reinforce the identity of Casablanca Coffees. Customers may choose from such offerings as Sam's Select, Ingrid's Choice and Bogie's Blend. The "Here's Looking at You Kid" phrase is set into a seal which is affixed onto packages and gifts.

The design team's serious commitment to a cohesive image program, coupled with a tongue-in-cheek approach, has achieved a special spirit and flavor for both the Casablanca Coffees store and its products.

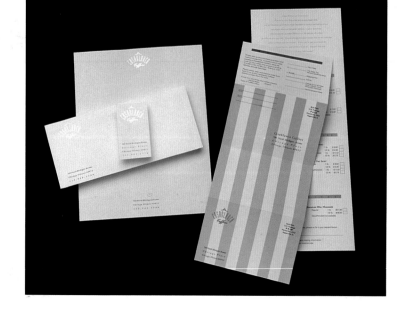

Design: *Schafer Associates, Inc., Oakbrook Terrace, IL*
Photographer: *Bob Briskey, Briskey Photography*

Architect: *Ronnette Riley Architect, New York, NY*
Principal: *Ronnette Riley, AIA*
Project Architect: *Dale Linden Turner, AIA*
Graphics: *Ronnette Riley Architect, AIA, New York, NY*
Real Design, New York, NY
Photographer: *Otto Baitz, Freehold, NJ*

New World Coffee was created to introduce a new world of superior, darker roasted, more flavorful coffees and espresso beverages to New York City.

The design mandate was to evoke the warmth of the experience and the aroma associated with coffee. This was accomplished by a dominant theme of coloration as well as a strong graphic identity that is reflected in the store's architectural layout as well as the logo.

To convey the aromatic and inviting feeling that comes with the enjoyment of coffee, the atmosphere was established by the selection of coppery earth tones …by use of ores and stone and wood. A green-gold backdrop, contrasted by cream colored walls and floor, generate a warm glow that is enhanced by overall lighting. To the customer passing the

technique ard — seemingly w.

offee is, itself, an sign. What had of the globe of the world ... eason of conspicuity, subjugated to a less important role. Instead, we see only a partial "world" — rising (with its warm rays) from the strong triangle shape. Why the triangle shape? Because that was the architectural floor plan. This measure of commitment by the architectural vocabulary to echo its voice through graphics has provided New World Coffee with its own signature triangle. Such a dominant symbol is quickly recognizable to consumers on coffee cups, packages and all related collateral.

PEABERRY COFFEE LTD.

Denver, Colorado

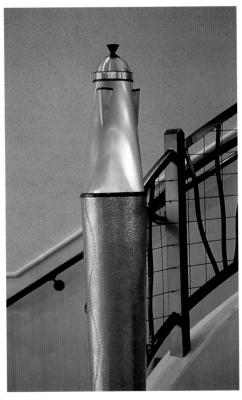

Recognizing that the wave of coffee popularity was swelling, Peaberry Coffee sought to find a brand identity of its own. The decision was made to take a cozy, welcoming approach — somewhat in contrast with those competitors who reflected a sleek, European look.

Partaking of coffee at Peaberry is an experience not unlike enjoying coffee in the kitchen. There's a warmth, a friendliness in both the architectural and interior design. Imagery suggesting a warm steamy "cuppa" extends from the coffee-inspired color scheme (ochre and tan) to a collection of coffee-inspired abstractions, graphically but subliminally incorporated into the shop's design. High above the entry way hangs a Paul Bunyan sized Peaberry coffee cup — a monumental gesture to the premium coffee and homey atmosphere that lies below.

The front patio, surrounded with a railing of metal tubing that's bent in steamy waves, is a motif that's meant to suggest the wafting of coffee aroma. Inside, cookware-metals (copper, bronze, stainless steel) that reflect a kitchen image are used in all sorts of imaginative ways: on counter tops, to cover ceiling beams, on structural trims. Most unique are the metallic sculptures — whimsical "monuments" to coffee drinking. There are several cast bronze coffee beans plus a statuesque four-spouted coffee pot that tops the banister post at the foot of the cafe's stairway.

The Peaberry logo, the warm hearth-like colors and the wafting-steam motif find their way onto all Peaberry products, labels and packaging. The kaffeeklatsch attitude is graphically translated— reinforcing the company image and successfully achieving an integrated, cohesive identity for this Colorado coffee retailer.

Identity/Interior Design: *Communication Arts, Boulder, CO*
Architect: *Blue Sky Studios, Denver, CO*
Theme Sculptures: *Colorado Instruments*
Photographer: *Galen Nathanson*

The Roast

	1/2 POUND	POUND		1/2 POUND	POUND			1/2 POUND	POUND
Guatemalan S.H.B.	4.20	7.45	Sulawesi	6.95	12.95	Peaberry's Special Blend		4.20	7.4
Brazil Bandeirante	4.10	7.25	Java Estate	4.70	8.45	Roaster's Choice		4.45	7.95
			Aged Sumatra	4.70	8.45	Flatiron Blend		4.70	8.45
Dark Roasts	1/2 POUND	POUND				Atlantic Pearl Blend		4.45	7.95
Viennese Blend	4.45	7.95	**Africa and Arabia**	1/2 POUND	POUND	**Flavored Decaf Coffees**		1/2 POUND	POUND
Espresso Milano	4.70	8.45	Kenya AA	4.70	8.45	Amaretto Almond Decaf		5.45	9.95
Espresso Roast	4.45	7.95	Mocha Yemen	6.45	11.95	Chocolate Raspberry and Cream Decaf		4.95	8.95
Sumatra	4.45	7.95	Tanzania Peaberry	4.45	7.95	French Vanilla Decaf		4.95	8.95
Dark French	4.45	7.95	Ethiopia Yergacheffe	5.20	9.45	Hazelnut Cream Decaf		4.95	8.95

Pure potential · Flavor unlocked · Character emerges · Patience, please · Supermarket style · Refinement begins · Flavor's peak · Aromatics glisten · Full power

Green · Yellow · Tan · Peanut · Cinammon Roast · City Roast · Full City Roast · Espresso Roast · French Roast

GIVE A GIFT
THAT KEEPS
ON GIVING.

JAVA EXPRESS

Northbrook, Illinois

Can you be a retail shop without having a physical location? Yes, you can, if you are a mobile kiosk or cart. Which makes the challenge for creating a retail image and graphic identity even all the more vital.

Java Express is a mobile coffee kiosk. (With plans to become mobile coffee kiosks — plural.) The design team's objective was, not only to create an identity that consumers would recognize — but to establish Java Express as so recognizable that potential investors in the company could see the opportunities for retail expansion.

Aiming at a target audience of discriminating (though hurried) coffee lovers who want a "cup to go", the Java Express conveys a very upscale image. It is artistically architectural in format— rendered in a sophisticated color combination of soft, rich wood tone contrasted with black. The custom-designed logo is set in reverse type — creating quick, easy readability and positive identification.

Kiosk/Graphic Design: *Schafer Associates, Inc., Oakbrook Terrace, IL*
Photographers: *Bob Briskey, Briskey Photography; John Boehm*

RETAIL GETAWAYS:
travel and leisure

I remember, some time ago, trying to put together a strong advertising team at Woodward & Lothrop — looking especially hard for a highly-credentialled media exec. Ultimately, I wooed someone away from an airline... and I remember being criticized by some as selecting a person who "didn't have retail experience". Retail experience? What could be more retail than an airline?

I think, today, the realization has arrived that filling seats on airlines, stadiums and theaters... putting bodies in beds... enticing art-lovers into museums and animal lovers into zoos — all, are very much retail!

This chapter spotlights a select handful of those in the travel and leisure industry who maximize their identities with strong, cohesive visual themes. Recognizable graphics, motifs, logos appear everywhere that is possible. On an aircraft's tail. On the floor of a cruise ship swimming pool. On a limousine door. On a bottle of fine wine. A billiard parlor called The Shark Club even goes so far as to bring its name to life — featuring live sharks swimming in giant tanks.

Travel. Leisure. Entertainment. You don't need a ticket to enjoy this tour. Just turn the page.

ALASKA AIRLINES

Seattle, Washington

Perhaps the smiling Eskimo face that graces the tails of Alaska Airlines jets has a reason to look pleased. He is not only one of the most identifiable images in travel, he also is now an integral part of one of the more successful image enhancement programs for an airline company.

The ethnic heritage of the state of Alaska provided the airlines' design team with the unique opportunity to convey a distinguishing visual point-of-view. The objective was to create a retail identity for Alaska Airlines that would be synonymous with "rugged", "youthful", "individualistic".

The first step was to give the airplanes, themselves, a new look. Along with the familiar

Eskimo icon, the planes were repainted to feature the stylized Alaska script — exploding the name into a 10-foot-tall sweep of letters that can easily be read from a block away.

Inside the planes — everything was redesigned — using the lore and character of the state of Alaska to communicate a singularly unique personality. Having drawn artistic inspiration from the themes of native Alaskan art, geometric patterns were created and woven into the the fabrics of seats, carpets and bulkheads. Food service items were redesigned, too — particularly appropriate for an airline that has a reputation for serving unusually good in-flight food. Sugar packets, paper cups, napkins, menus as well as the china in first class now boast the new design theme.

Flight schedules, playing cards, ticket jackets and stationery also carry the graphic identity. Even flight attendants' uniforms have been included in the identity overhaul. Absolutely everything delivers the airlines' new look, conveying a clear message: this is Alaska Airlines!

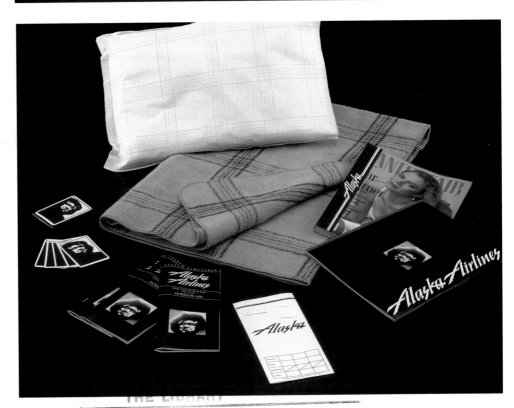

Designer:
Seattle Design Group, Seattle, WA
Photographers:
Robert Vinnedge, James Aronovsky, Todd Pearson

Architect:

Michael Graves, Architect, Princeton, NJ

Photographers:

Anne Garrison/David Hewitt, San Diego, CA

The Hyatt Regency at Aventine has an identity of its own — distinct and apart from the corporate Hyatt identity. Its individualism speaks with one of America's important architectural voices, that of Michael Graves.

It can be argued that the hotel's Italianate neoclassicism is more Graves than Hyatt. But then, since that is exactly the ingredient that makes the hotel identifiable, familiar and memorable to guests, the Aventine location qualifies eminently for a position in this book.

The Aventine is actually a mixed-use site — visually striking in the way its thematic architecture is translated into an 11-story office building, a health club, four restaurants and the 400-room Hyatt Regency. The different geometric shapes of the buildings create a powerful composition, forming a "campus" of circles, squares and pergolas.

Reinforcing the geometric theme, the Hyatt features gridded windows that are set in slightly from the facade. For travellers, exiting from California's freeway #5, the building is literally a landmark.

The grid theme reappears in several translations throughout the interior of the hotel. The lobby restaurant features a spectacular oversized gridded window. No ordinary chairs surround the cocktail tables: the exclusive chair back design repeats the window-pane graphic. Throughout, there are Graves-designed rugs. Tall marble columns guide guests through a dramatic but dignified lobby of grand scale: two stories high.

The compelling composition resulting from the designer's idiosyncratic translation of geometrics into architecture, is equally recognizable in the small scale pieces designed by Graves. Some are sold in the hotel's gift shop; many others are offered through the Graves Design Collection catalog.

MARRIOTT'S DESERT SPRINGS RESORT & SPA

Palm Desert, California

Seasoned travelers know this hotel as the one with the boat in the lake in the lobby! If ever there was an image of an oasis in the desert, Marriott's Desert Springs Resort is the quintessential hideaway.

Its architectural design is lavish. Low, gracefully proportioned buildings overlook lush gardens and mountain vistas. Guests are spellbound by the incredible marble lobby — from whence one descends, stepping between little waterfalls to the indoor "dock" to board the canopied boat for a sail. Giant doors open automatically and the boat moves outdoors. The "captain" points out the golf courses as well as the hotel's luxury features and amenities for arriving guests. In the evenings, the boat transports diners to either of three international restaurants, Mikado, Tuscany or Sea Grille.

Hovering everywhere throughout Marriott's resort and spa is the Desert Springs hummingbird. As if to monitor the pleasure of each guest, this beautiful motif is "in flight" on the tennis courts, golf courses, at the spa, at dining and cocktail locations and in all the guest bathrooms — alighting on everything from tennis visors to plush terry robes, from golf bags to cosmetics. The hummingbird insignia is hardly out of sight. As a design motif, it was appropriately chosen as the resort's symbol because it represents energy in motion and captures the iridescent color of the desert.

Every article of printed stationery or travel literature that is given or sent by Marriott's Desert Springs Resort & Spa features the hummingbird motif. This whimsical creature is never absent, and makes such a strong statement, that it successfully stands alone as the recognizable graphic identity for the resort.

Architects: *Killingsworth, Stricker, Lindgren, Wilson & Associates, Los Angeles, CA*
Photography: *Jim Burtnett*

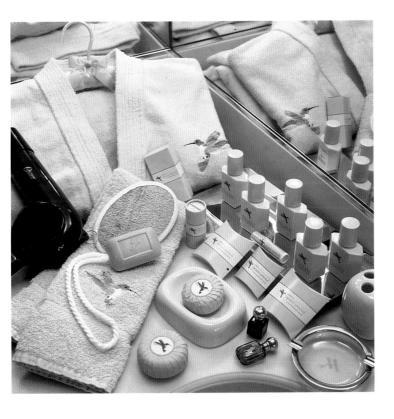

HOTEL HANKYU INTERNATIONAL

Osaka, Japan

To carry a Hotel Hankyu International luggage tag on one's briefcase is to display a discriminating taste for choosing the best.

The hotel is the flagship luxury hotel of the Hankyu Corporation Group, a conglomerate of 305 diversified business. The Group is one of Japan's leading railway companies and is active in the real estate, retailing and leisure industries.

Standard operating procedure for development of most hotel projects is to determine the architecture first, and then follow with the graphic program. Interestingly, in this case, the decision was to commission the identity program before any other design project. And thus, the graphic elements which were created were used to guide in the development of the hotel's interior and architecture.

The objective was carefully articulated: "to develop a distinctive emblem that would communicate quality, internationalism and the universal appeal of flowers."

The result: a system of six stylized flower symbols — one for each floor, and a custom alphabet to be used with them. The concept was to express luxury by differentiating items in the hotel with special details.

A traveler's first encounter with the flower symbol is immediate — upon driving (or taxi-ing) in! The image is truly a stunner. The beautiful graphics are faithfully portrayed on signage, room folders, stationery, menus and — most exquisitely, on the amenities found in every room.

For business or pleasure travelers who fly in or out of Japan's new international airport, the Hotel Hankyu International has established an image and identity that accurately reflects its opulence.

Graphics Design Program: *Michael Gericke, Colin Forbes, Pentagram, New York, NY*
Collaborating Design Team: *OUN Design Corp. & Dentsu Inc., Tokyo, Japan*
Interior Design: *Intradesign, Los Angeles, CA*

PRINCESS CRUISES

THE LOVE BOAT

It's more than just a ship… it's the Loveboat. Is there anyone who doesn't know we're talking about Princess Cruises?

The company has been enormously successful in keeping its name highly recognizable in the travel market because it has maintained a communications program that is strategically consistent.

From a visual perspective, the image of the princess' head with her graceful flowing hair provides immediate "brand recognition", even when used without the name Princess Cruises. This achievement is a result of the company's commitment to present the princess logo at every opportunity — making sure that consumers never forget who she is and whom she represents.

It was at the time the company launched its first ship, the Princess Patricia in 1968, that the princess logo was created. The artistic assignment was to create an emblem that connoted grace and femininity (as ships are referred to in this gender). It was also to capture a sense of movement, thereby symbolizing the ocean waves.

Today, this lovely logo has become a familiar face. Most dramatically, it is positioned on the stack of each Princess Cruises ship. (An interesting note: the hair is always shown flowing in the proper direction as the ship moves through the water.)

Passengers aboard a Princess ship will encounter the logo on signage, newsletters, serving ware, terry robes, amenity packs, etc. A particularly enchanting representation of the Princess logo is found painted on the bottom of the swimming pool.

Remembrances of Princess Cruises adventures are important to travellers. And so a large collection of gift merchandise has been developed. Coffee mugs, waterglobes, photo albums, tote bags, golf umbrellas, T-shirts, hats and license plate frames are examples of merchandise with the princess identity — filling the need for both collecting and recollecting special memories.

MUSEO DE ARTE CONTEMPORANEO

Monterrey, Nueva Leon, Mexico

The acronym for Museo de Arte Contemporaneo is MARCO — which also happens to be the Spanish word for frame. How intriguing that the concept of the frame as a geometric form has literally shaped the identity of the facility.

Both the architectural design of the museum and the environmental graphics are in total unison — truly framing a distinctive personality. The museum building is itself a "frame" — designed around a square central patio. In addition to framing the patio, the architecture frames itself, with squares cut in walls to allow views of other walls.

The visitor encounters the identity of MARCO the moment he approaches the museum's entrance: sculpted into the wall is the name MARCO with its protruding graphic square "O". Decorative exterior square flags bear the signature square opening. Stepping inside the lobby, one encounters the information desk which is …yes,a perfect square of travertine.

The "frame" reappears in the signing throughout the museum — cutout square travertine "hoops" designate exhibits spaces, restrooms, the gift shop.

Promotional print materials such as invitations to museum events feature square die-cuts and foldouts to reinforce MARCO's graphic image, conveying the identity of the museum to readers in their homes even when the the building is nowhere in sight. The gift shopping

bags, also, carry the graphic message. To imitate the square hole, the bags have a clear plastic center, framed by the opaque solid color of the rest of the bag.

MARCO is a tribute to the extraordinary collaboration of both architecture and graphic design to achieve one dramatic identity.

Architect: *Ricardo Legoretta, Legorreta Arquitectos, Mexico City*
Environmental Graphic Designer: *Lance Wyman, Denise Guerra, Lance Wyman Ltd., New York, NY*
Photographer: *Lance Wyman*

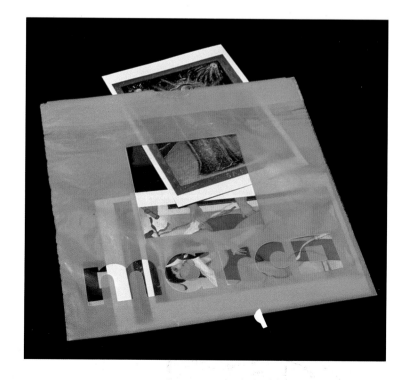

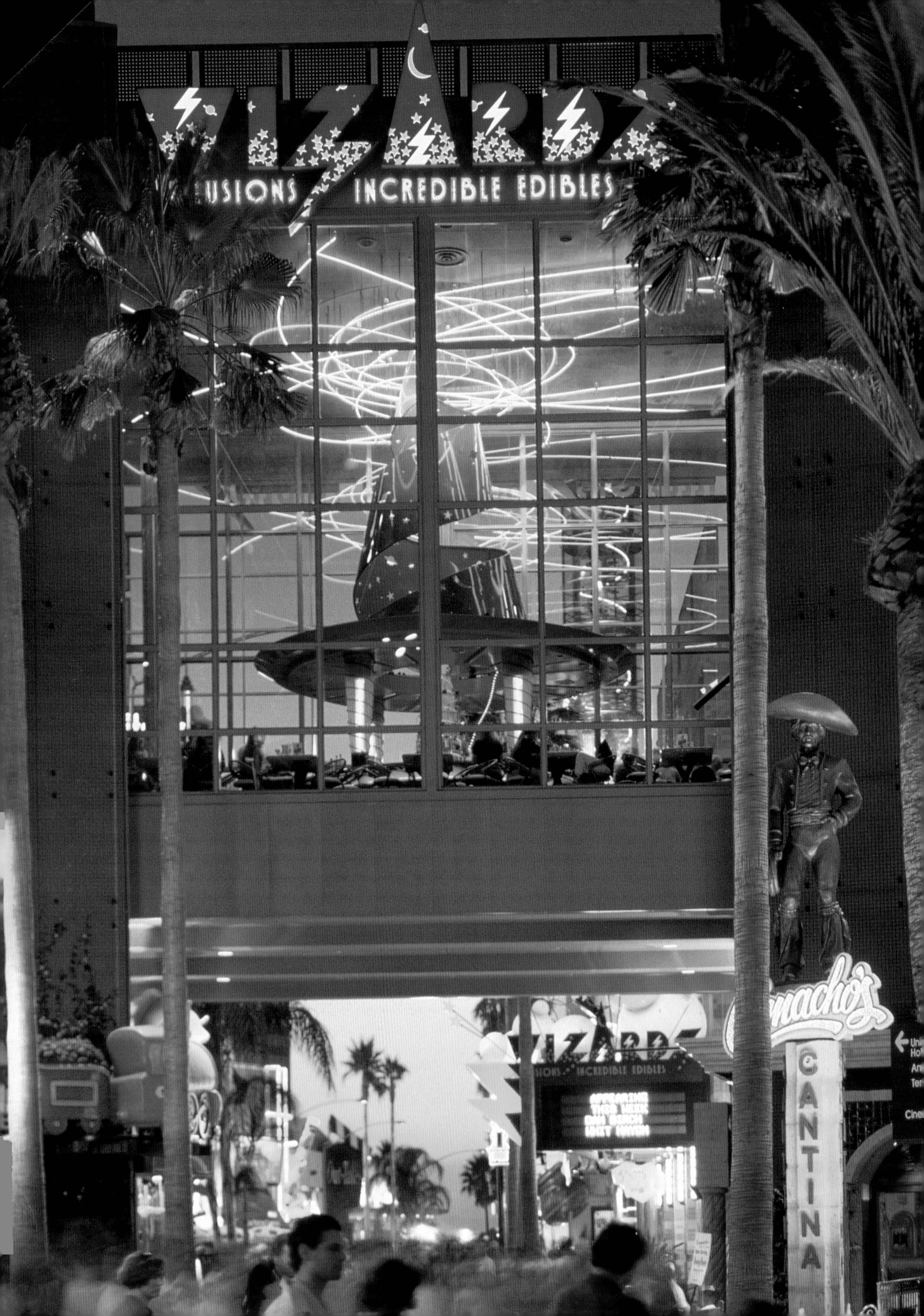
WIZARDZ
ILLUSIONS INCREDIBLE EDIBLES
CANTINA

If you think this retailer is just a lot of hocus pocus, look again. Relegated to a second story location, Wizardz needed to try twice as hard to entice customers to come to their private magic club.

Abracadabra… they started by creating a logo of lightning bolt letters — complete with stars and "z's". Across the top of the building, the letters are 4-to-8-feet-tall. The theater marquee features the same celestial logo — this time, illuminated and burping polycarbonate bubbles.

The second floor facade is constructed of glass panes, allowing the street crowd to catch a glimpse of the neon lights orbiting the mammoth conical Merlin hat that dominates the interior design in the magic theater upstairs.

Tempted by the exterior graphics, customers are not disappointed when they step inside to board the elevator to the second floor. "Airport lights" track the elevators location. And above the doorway messages like "levitate" and "arise" set the mood for the magic to come.

Once inside the magic theater, guests are treated to a hi-tech celestial environment! The stage is lined with illuminated lightning bolts that flash, pulse and dim as visual punctuation to the magic show on stage.

High above the room's jazzy star-studded tables (a Merlin hat atop each one) the ceiling twinkles mysteriously. Even the carpeting has been custom-designed to echo the theme.

The integration of graphic images at Wizardz is retail theater at its best. The visual messages go wherever the customers go. To the rest rooms. On the street outside where a costumed Merlin acts as barker. This is identity collaboration made in designer's heaven.

Design Consultants and Environmental Graphics: *Communication Arts, Boulder, CO*
Architect: *Hirata Architects, Los Angeles, CA*
Photographers: *Grey Crawford and Communication Arts*

RAND MC NALLY

Chicago, Illinois

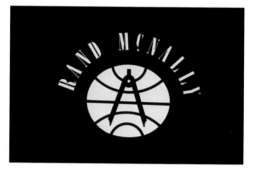

Retail Design and Graphics:
Fitch, Inc., Columbus, Ohio

If you ask for a synonym for "Rand McNally" … expect a response like "map" or "globe". This famous publisher and retailer of maps has its traditional roots in catering to the business and educational segments of the population.

Recognizing that the market for travel shopping has now broadened (appealing to the general populace), Rand McNally has moved into the retail arena in a serious manner, creating stores that entice shoppers by dramatically conveying the romance and adventure of travel within traditional-cum-contemporary surroundings.

A careful choice of fixturing design, materials, fabrications and lighting provide an environment not unlike a library. The objective is to invite browsing. With today's travelers being more mobile, more sophisticated and possessed of a higher degree of geographic literacy, the opportunity to search and research at leisure serves as a real incentive for customers to come inside.

The graphic design of the store has actually been built into the architecture. The dramatic and familiar Rand McNally compass mark welcomes the visitor at the door; on the floor of the entryway, the logo is inlaid in mosaic.

Books and maps and travel tapes are grouped by geographical location, rather than by categories, which has a visual impact on increasing the time a customer spends in the store.

Signage throughout the store has been created to capture the feeling of old documents. The Rand McNally compass mark logo is incorporated into the signage and is also used wherever the opportunity presents itself. It appears on shopping bags, map tubes, wrapping paper, brochures, stationery — completing the defining image of the travel retailer.

THREE OUTRAGEOUS POOL PARLORS

Gotham Hall, Metropolis, The Shark Club
Southern California

Minnesota Fats would have loved playing his beloved pool at Gotham Hall, Metropolis or The Shark Club. At each of these "pool parlors" the cue games can be enjoyed in environments that turn a mere sporting event into an evening of fun and entertainment.

Each club has its own theatrical identity: three different places of panache — each one created to be clearly distinctive and unquestionably memorable.

Gotham Hall is the hot spot in Santa Monica. It's a billiard club richly designed with modern materials and colors. Intense tones of purple, green and terra cotta adorn the walls and are accentuated with metallic touches. Avant-garde furnishings add style as does the overscaled checkerboard carpet inlay pattern. The neo-Gothic logo is combined with several design elements, including iron sculpture, to portray Gotham's identity on everything from menus to matchbooks.

Retail Design: *Hatch Design Group, Costa Mesa, CA*
Graphics: *On the Edge, Newport Beach, CA*
Photographers: *Ron Pollard, Scott Rothwell, Martin Fine*

Soups and Salads

Calamari Salad   7.50
Enoki Mushroom Salad   7.50
Miso Soup   2.50
Salmon Skin Salad

Rolls

California Roll   5.00
Caterpillar Roll   7.50
_____ mber Roll
_____ ow Roll
_____ n Roll
_____ eam cheese, le__
_____ s Pizza B_____
_____ Tuna R____
_____ ta Ro____
_____ ll

METROPOLIS

"One man's symbolism is another man's technology."

Terence McKenna

Pool

Sushi

Dancing

Grill

You and a guest are invited

to attend a private party celebrating
the opening of Metropolis.

Date: Tuesday, September 29, 1992

Time: 7:30 – ?

Place: Metropolis
4255 Campus Dr. Irvine
714-725-0300

405 Freeway

Please detach & present

Metropolis, in Costa Mesa, is brimming with drama. Its design is "retro"-inspired and translates as an offbeat version of a 1920's club. The character of the space begins at the entry, where an undulating metal-paneled wall leads past the oversized harlequin ceiling. Purple and gold pop out dominantly against black. There's an interesting counterpoint of the stark type design and logo against the voluptuousness of Roman-like classic artwork. From the environment to the matchbooks and chopstick wrappers, Metropolis is mesmerizing.

And then there's The Shark Club. Yes, there ARE sharks— real live Black Tipped sharks, swimming in a huge 2,000 gallon tank in the middle of this billiard emporium in Irvine. Patrons who schedule an early evening game enjoy the thrill of feeding these awesome sea creatures. No surprise that the club's graphics on their collateral features a "Jaws-like" photograph. The best adjective for this unique retail establishment is surely "unforgettable."

LA COSTA RESORT AND SPA

Carlsbad, California

When the chauffered limousine pulls in at the airport to meet arriving guests, everyone recognizes the prestigious "LC" logo on the door. La Costa Resort and Spa is internationally known as a preeminent spa, golf and tennis resort. And despite the increase in health and fitness resorts both here and abroad, La Costa has established a legendary identity.

Located on 400 acres in one of the most fertile gardening areas in southern California, La Costa takes advantage of nature's bounty to emblazon its familiar "LC" in beds of incredibly colorful flowers.

With two championship golf courses, La Costa hosts 75,000 rounds each year — among them, the PGA Tour's annual Mercedes Championships. No wonder guests proudly wear the La Costa logo on golf shirts and visors. Ardent tennis players (there are 21 courts) also sport the La Costa logo on their attire.

At the Spa, health therapies are not the only wonderful things that envelope the guests. Everywhere, the La Costa graphic identity is quietly pervasive. The pristine white La Costa terry wrap has become a coveted robe. And the comprehensive range of La Costa spa products has become a major business unto itself — now successfully marketed via catalog. La Costa-labeled products are recognized and purchased by many who have never visited the resort but recognize the name, the identity, the image.

Fun and games. That's what Circo Porto is all about. And that is exactly what the design team successfully communicated via their imaginative approach to architecture and graphics.

Circo Porto is an adult arcade gallery and eating center. It's a a place created to provide an evening of quality fun for adults who like to play with video and games.

In order to capture the spirit of the arcade/gallery which is located within a harbor by the sea, the designers used metals, neon, acrylic paints, paper and fabric to achieve the retail setting. To identify the the harbor location, a "water graphic" was incorporated into the logo. A red wave is the base of the logo… and floating above it is a smiling crescent-moon-face and and a star to dot the "i".

The Circo Porto logo truly tells a story; it clearly communicates evening fun. And to make sure customers don't forget that message, the graphic identity finds its way in neon, at the entranceway and in print — on menus, brochures, matchbook covers and on promotional giveaways.

Design Firm: *Profile Design, San Francisco, CA*
Architect/Art Director: *Konichi Nishiwaki*

ORIENT-EXPRESS HOTELS, INC.

London, England

The Orient-Express! Just breathing the words conjures up exotic images of faraway lands, of mysterious voyages and, for those of us who are fans of Agatha Christie — adventure!

The identity (and the journey) begin when boarding the train. Faithfully restored to their legendary stature, each of the carriages bears the company's dramatic signature emblem. Whether a passenger's destination takes him aboard the shining green Eastern & Oriental Express or the magnificent blue and gold wagon-lits carriages of the Venice Simplon-Orient-Express, the character of the railway remains omnipresent.

Uniforms for car conductors, waiters, baggage carriers, etc. have been designed to recreate the original costumes. The company logo appears wherever good taste dictates: on beautiful leather goods, silk scarves, accessories. The gift shop features 1930 train posters and miniature model trains. All passengers receive the highly stylized Orient-Express Magazine, along with coveted mementos like logo soap and the distinguished writing paper.

Throughout the cars (the opulent piano bar, the dining cars, the compartments) the interior decor meticulously reflects the image of the era. Adornments include marquetry panels, Art Deco lamps and Lalique-like glass panels etched with the Orient-Express insignia.

What makes the Orient-Express' image so extraordinary is that the development of its character has been accomplished as much through the ambiance of the "experience" as through the design identity.

STERLING VINEYARDS®

ESTATE GROWN & BOTTLED

1992

Sauvignon

For anyone journeying to the crescent-shaped Napa Valley in northern California, a visit to Sterling Vineyards is a "must". It is not simply that this is among the state's finest wineries… it is also the magnificence of the edifice, itself, which has gained a worldwide reputation. Because of its distinctive architecture, the facility's design has set the visual theme for everything that identifies Sterling.

The white monastic buildings of Sterling Vineyards sit majestically on a knoll, some 300 feet high, overlooking the entire Napa Valley. Access is via an aerial tramway. Veiled in morning fog, starkly white against storm clouds or turned pale rose by a deepening valley sunset, Sterling seems at first glance more an exotic Mediterranean village than a winery. (The Ionian architectural style widely found in the Greek island of Mykonos was the source of the theme used.)

It is no surprise that the impactful and memorable image of the winery was chosen as the primary graphic "symbol". The "portrait" of the winery as it sits commandingly on the bluff, is the art for the wine bottle labels. A further graphic translation of the winemaker imagery is the grape leaf: a theme used on brochures, in-store promotion displays and racks, bottle neck hangers, folders, stationery, etc.

For those who have toured Sterling Vineyards, the design identity provides immediate recognition in the wine stores. For those who have not … the integrated visual imagery is surely an enticement.

Architect:

Martin Waterfield

Graphics Design:

Sally Cohn, Pickett Communications,
San Francisco, CA

Photographers:

Michel Rabaste Photography, Stephen Zanelli

OMNIUM-GATHERUM:
a surprising diversity of retailers

This chapter of miscellany truly speeds its way from A to Z! It's a compendium of creative retailers — running the gamut from an art store in Japan to a Zebra-inspired copy shop.

Classifying this visual cacophony of stores was not only an impossibility, but it also seemed to homogenize the magic of the mix.

In this chapter, you will find so many wonderful picture-stories. All kinds of different retailers — from stores that feed the mind and soul to one where the eyes have it! There's a shop where the game is everything… and one with a degree of academia. Another boutique celebrates its city. And, at NASA, there's an infinite inventory of mementos of America's space missions.

Geographically, this chapter has its diversity, too. Do you have the time to travel to Tokyo? Or Puerto Rico? Or how about East Grinstead, West Sussex, England? We take you on those journeys and we have no doubt… they are trips that will be enjoyable and enlightening.

Retail Concept: *Tony & Joni Goldstein, Toronto, CAN*
Interior Design and Graphics: *International Design Group, Toronto, CAN*
Photographers: *Robert Burley, Design Archive; Jim Dawson, Fotowork*

OH YES TORONTO

Ja! Hi! Si! Mais oui! However one says it, international travelers exclaim "Oh Yes Toronto!" Clearly a most appropriate name for this unique retailer of quality souvenir merchandise, it also successfully attracts a local clientele.

What makes the shop so attention-getting is the big, bright yellow exclamation mark that is emblazoned everywhere. It punctuates the character of the store as well as the excitement of the city it represents. From a graphic point of view, it is wonderfully appealing and easily identifiable.

Approaching the unadorned glass storefront, the customer's gaze is immediately captured by the imaginative ceiling: an oversized floating sloped logo T-shirt. Other versions of the logo T-shirt (which is, of course, sold in the shop) appears on walls and on displays — creating an inherent signage program of its own.

Hurried travellers find it difficult to rush through this well-displayed, well-merchandised shop. They can make selections ranging from wearables to mugs, pens to frisbees. And then they carry out their purchases in attractive Oh Yes Toronto shopping bags or boxes.

It's hardly surprising to find that the company stationery and business cards also are graphically exclamatory. Consistency is a watchword with Oh Yes Toronto. As the chain expands, they continually reinforce not only the vitality of the city, but their own strong identity as well. Oh yes indeed!

UCLA SPIRIT

Universal City, California

No… it is not the abominable snowman's print. The giant cast impression of a 4x5 foot paw that greets you on the stone floor at the entry to this shop is that of Bruin — the mascot of the University of California Los Angeles (familiarly known as UCLA).

And this is Bruin's shop: UCLA SPIRIT. Unorthodox in location as well as in retail concept, this shop makes a play to an audience beyond its college campus, bringing the essence of the popular southern California university lifestyle to tourists and the community at large. It is presented as a colorful melange of nostalgic and state-of-the-art technology.

To translate the distinctive architecture of the UCLA campus, the design team "recreated" the Romanesque arches and bas relief details on the store's facade. Further, they adapted elements of that architectural motif throughout the interior. The school's colors, blue and yellow, are integrated into the design (even the carpeting is "UCLA blue") and brightly spotlighted in neon at the entry.

The bear symbol is as much a part of the interior design as it is as a logo theme for an incredible line of merchandise. There are T-shirts, sweatshirts, hats and other casual apparel for children and adults as well as license plate holders, back packs, tote bags and jewelry along with all kinds of textbook supplies. The bruin stuffed animals are everyone's favorites — ranging in size from tot-sized toys to giant huggables.

Far from looking academic, the UCLA Spirit shop bearly conveys just what its name says, "spirit" — the spirit of contemporary college life.

Store Design and Graphics: Phyllis Schultz, Steven Kelso
ASUCLA: Associated Students, UCLA, Los Angeles, CA

INCREDIBLE UNIVERSE

A Division of Tandy Corporation, Fort Worth, Texas

One visit to Incredible Universe, and you know the future is now! The design team for this mammoth high-tech retailer has devised the space to capture an energized environment of advanced technologies — providing its customers with the ultimate destination store.

Spanning the length of two football fields, this prototype store, located in Portland, Oregon, mesmerizes shoppers with its "star trek" presentation of televisions, VCR's, camcorders and home appliances. Color, lights, neon, strobes — everywhere. There are laser light shows, a karaoke studio, photo developing and a video editing lab. A huge "event" rotunda marks the center core where on-going entertainment is provided for shoppers — from the fun of a disc jockey booth to music videos and movies projected on jumbo multi-media screens.

The thematic graphic for Incredible Universe is an infinite sky with its shooting stars and comets. This visual motif is all-pervasive — from the retailer's interior to membership cards and shopping bags to shirts and hats. Signage is bigger than life — purposely overscaled and whimsical to reinforce the big, free, feeling of fun and pleasure. Incredible Universe has even found a way to transport its image to customers' homes! Their eye-catching delivery trucks deliver their image and identity as well as their merchandise!

In light of the reality that retailing is part show-business, part merchandising… Incredible Universe has successfully achieved an identity as both!

Retail Design: *Scott Smith, Carolyn Zudell, Design Forum, Dayton, OH*
Architect: *Design Forum Architects*
Photographer: *Strode-Eckert*

KODAK'S RAHOLA IMAGE CENTER

Ponce, Puerto Rico

Designer: *Marc Gobé, Kenneth Hirst, Cato Gobé & Associates, New York*
Architect: *José Toro, Underwood Architects*
Photographer: *Andrew Bordwin*

Kodak is a name known around the world. One can buy Kodak photographic products in many kinds of shops running the gamut from convenience stores to tourist kiosks. But with the creation of this new Rahola Image Center, there is now a single retail destination where the world of Kodak comes alive. Kodak's acquisition of the Rahola chain of film processing stores in Latin America reflects a commitment to create an environment to specifically reflect the wonders of the art of picture-taking.

With the design of the new Rahola store in Ponce, Puerto Rico, Kodak has launched an exciting new prototype for an innovative new retail concept. Rahola isn't just an outlet for photoprocessing and equipment. By its very design, Rahola emerges from the laboratory-like photo store category to become a visual world of discovery. The atmosphere is emo-tional, not technical. The store environment is a world of "imaging" with enticing department designations and interactive opportunities for customers. Rather than departments, customers visit individual zones which are easily identifiable by huge, brightly colored backdrops topped by film-sprocket graphics. And, in lieu of the commonplace department signs, there are informal designations and fun photos. Rather than "camera department", a friendly script says "Capture". Instead of "black and white film", a customer comes upon a giant photo of a zebra.

Another important design statement is made as result of the color choices for Rahola's facade and interior decor. The dynamic (and very recognizable) yellow/gold, red and black of Kodak products dominate the store. Even the Rahola name has been designed to mimic the familiar typestyle of "Kodak".

Few retailers enjoy the "parenting" of so strong a consumer franchise as Kodak. The Rahola design has ingeniously capitalized on that image of leadership, at the same time, creating a dynamic identity of its own.

UVU BY RCA

This story has more to do with retail "things" than retail "places". However, the comprehensiveness of the program to develop a recognizable identity for the product was such an intimate partnership of client and designer that this is a tale worth telling.

We're talking about an RCA television set radically different in design, with an amorphous cabinet featuring softened rounded edges. The graphic designer and the client sought to create a name for the set — one that would evoke an idea for developing a strong typographic identity and/or logo. Thus evolved the name "UVU" — readable as "you view", and, at the same time, representing the initials for Unconventional Video Unit. And with this idea came the design concept of making all graphic elements of packaging relate to the television and the UVU logo.

Since a consumer shopping for a television set is besieged by a floor cluttered with different models and different brands — and usually the display of cartons is even more overwhelming… the challenge was to create packaging that conveyed the concept of the UVU set inside.

The solution was the highly stylized UVU typography: short wide letters that formed a very contemporary and very eye-catching design. Cleverly, no matter how the UVU boxes are stacked, they create a point of sale display. The UVU logo is further employed on all inserts, instructional manuals, posters, POP and promotional materials — even on T-shirts for sales floor staff.

The relationship of the graphics program vis-a-vis the product design has been logically conceived. The product, the image and identity: all are one.

Graphic Design:
Paula Scher, Pentagram Design Inc., New York, NY
Photographer:
William Whitehurst

GTE TELEPHONE OPERATIONS

Customer Service Center
Tampa, Florida

The customer contact center for conducting telephone business need not be dull and stodgy. In fact, it shouldn't be, if there's to be pleasant and effective interaction between consumers and representatives.

To this end, the design team for GTE Telephone Operations sought to make the service center new, different and stimulating. Partly this involved space design. But it also involved attitude design — providing a reinvigorating employee zones where employees could take breaks, relax and unwind so they'd be fresh and rejuvenated in order to interact positively and energetically

with customers. Those two zones include the physical break/exercise area and the Cafe News Bar.

Throughout the GTE Telephone Operations center, the color scheme is wake-up bright — a relief from the often-tired monotone colors of hi-tech offices. Bright navy blue and yellow/gold appear throughout the graphics, on signs, banners and on architectural elements. In the Cafe News Bar, the addition of vibrant red on bar stools, chairs and banquettes adds to the environment's lively attitude and image.

Design Firm: *Robert Turner, Turner Design, New York, NY*

GREG'S BODY SHOP

Joliet, Illinois

2419 W. JEFFERSON ST. • JOLIET, IL 60435 • 815.741.4244

If an automotive repair retailer sounds like an unlikely candidate to represent the concept of design and graphic image... Greg's Auto Body Shop is probably an exception to the rule.

The very reality that automative shops are both common and common-looking became the challenge for this retailer, who sought to rise above the clutter and achieve an image that reflected quality, professionalism and service.

The logo that was created for Greg's Body Shop became a hallmark for the company. The symbol is reminiscent of the emblems of classic automotive marques and it conveys an upscale identity. It immediately makes a statement about Greg's

and definitely and distinctively sets this retailer apart from the general category of auto repair. Even the color scheme is rich: a combination of metallic red, gold and black.

The bold, contemporary awning makes an introductory statement; it forms a customer's first impression. From there on, the logo continues to emerge and repeat the retailer's name and identity. Service representatives wear logo shirts, logo jackets, logo caps — even logo watches.

A whole range of premium items have been developed: pens and frisbees, lighters and magnets and coffee cups. For one shop to embark on merchandising of this scope clearly indicates the retailer's commitment to establish a "top-of-mind" awareness.

This powerful identity program has not only accomplished its purpose in terms of providing customers with a high perception of Greg's Body Shop, it has also succeeded in instilling a new sense of pride for the retailer's entire staff.

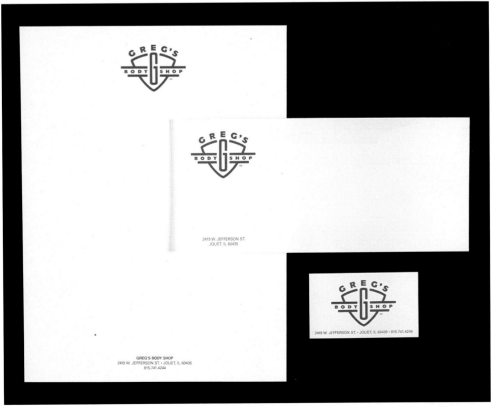

Design/Graphics: *Bullet Communications, Inc., Joliet, IL*

ARTHUR HAYES OPTOMETRISTS

East Grinstead, West Sussex, England

In the south of England, in a charming old 16th century building, there resides an optician whose retail store is truly a "site for sore eyes."

This East Grinstead branch of the UK-based independent chain of Arthur Hayes Optometrists has, by virtue of an integrated program of visual design, defined itself as emphatically different from the run-of-the-mill optometric establishments.

The renovation of the building, the stunning redesign of the interior (both spatially and decoratively) along with a distinctive new graphic identity serves to capture and communicate its exceptionally high standard of service and their technical authority.

The interior environment of the store has been devised — not only to be beautiful, but also to be more functional. Space design actually simplifies the customer transaction; people are "filtered" from one attractive area to another— from waiting area to consulting area to a fashionable eyeglass selection area.

And talk about eyecatching! The logo script is truly a work of "signature" art, taking its bows along with the stylized "eyeglass" art. This identity is etched onto the glass of the store window and then is further implemented on all point-of-sale material as well as on their

letterhead, business cards, appointment cards (and accompanying wallet holder), note cards, stickers and shopping bags.

Here is an excellent example of a comprehensive program of visual design that intelligently and attractively communciates the exceptionally high-quality of Arthur Hayes' merchandise and service. The design team's collaboration has successfully given this retailer a look all its own!

Interior Design and Retail Graphics: *Fitch, London, England*
Photographer: *Bruce Hennings*

SCRIBNER'S

A Division of B. Dalton, New York, New York

The venerable Scribner's book shop on Manhattan's Fifth Avenue is no more. But despite the demise of that longtime location, Scribner's, the bookseller, is alive and well and expanding its presence in contemporary mall sites.

What is most impressive about the "new" Scribner's shops is that they manage to look and feel much like the old Scribner's. The design team has brilliantly adapted those proprietary architectural and graphic elements that were so much in the Scribner's design vernacular and "reconditioned" them with a smart, contemporary flair.

For example, the entryway to the store is rendered in black and brass and portrays a stylized, simplified rendition of the legendary New York facade. The broken pediment over the entrance arch reappears as a decorative motif through the interior space.

A smart new program of graphics has also been developed to increase the retailer's visibility. LIke the navy blue and gold of the store facade, these two colors are used everywhere. The "Scribner's" logo always appears in gold, like the highly polished brass letters above the door. The lamp of learning that has long been associated with Scribner's has been stylishly adapted and appears as an overall motif on the stunning navy blue shopping bags, as well as on stationery, cards, bookmarks, brochures and interior signage. Across the board, the Scribner's retail image program has been well-conceived and well-coordinated, successfully combining time-honored design characteristics from the past with a crisp, updated image of the 90's.

Retail Store Design & Graphics: *SDI-HTI, New York, NY*

PREMIER BANK

New Orleans, Louisiana

If you hadn't thought of it before, banks are nothing but retail shops for money. They provide financial services of all kinds to consumers — and as such, they are as challenged as fashion stores to emerge from a crowded, competitive marketplace.

Premier Bank recognized this reality and aggressively sought to establish its own unique personality. Boldly and uncharacteristically, it looked to make a splash; and it has. At its "branch of the future" all sorts of visual messages combine to create a retail banking environment that is different and clearly recognizable to its target audience of busy professionals.

No mausoleum-like grey marble or iron-cages here; instead, bold saturated colors give the bank a lively, upbeat atmosphere. The center-piece is an enormous "art" rug. Derived from a painting by a local artist, the rug incorporates elements that visually describe the spirit of the city of New Orleans. Motifs from the rug's design recur on invitations and handouts as well as on striking outdoor banners that feature the slogan "Dreams/Ideals/Prosperity."

In the style of the best retailers, Premier Bank employs its windows as a selling tool. An enormous seal of excellence has been designed and it appears, as if in "etched glass" on windows in sizes up to 20 feet. This arresting graphic features a giant "E" and the statement "Everyday Excellence", which is cleverly repeated on appropriate advertising materials throughout the bank.

This extraordinary departure from the usual "bank look" has successfully differentiated Premier Bank, giving it a dynamic and cosmopolitan identity as well as a critical edge over competition.

Architect: *Sizeler Architects, Baton Rouge, LA*
Retail Design and Strategy: *Fitch, Inc., Columbus, OH*
Environmental Graphic Design: *DSI/LA, Baton Rouge, LA*

FRANKLIN QUEST

Salt Lake City, Utah

Using a style that they refer to as "Neo-Colonial" the design team devised storefronts with stature — making a dramatic and impressive statement by way of massive architectural columns.

The team also realized that the store interior design demanded an approach that communicated an organized layout. Customers would need to perceive that Franklin Quest projected itself as a company that was qualified to train them to organize their lives. Solution: utilization of rich, dark woods and construction of library-like display units that are systematically arranged to separate "product" by section. With a great emphasis on packaging design, the groupings of Day Planners, binders, instructional tapes, etc. form a cohesive visual presentation of their own.

Besides the use of wood, marble was also chosen as a material that connotes quality. It is used not only as accents in architectural and interior design, but also finds its way onto collateral — such as the handsome logo shopping bag. Advantageously, the Ben Franklin logo is easily identifiable, and, as such, the company maximizes it by putting it onto ancillary materials like rulers, folders, hole punchers.

In his "Advice to a Young Tradesman" Benjamin Franklin espoused, "Remember that time is money." In view of that philosophy, it is appropriate that Franklin Quest, the time and life management company, has adopted Mr. Franklin's likeness as its symbol. (Even the company phone number honors him as a signer of the Declaration of Independence, employing 1776 as the last four digits.)

When Franklin Quest decided to enter the retail scene (after years of marketing their seminars and services through catalogs and direct sales) it became a clear challenge to design stores that would authenticate the mission of the company.

Architect:

Chris Layton, Smith Layton and Anderson,
Salt Lake City, UT

Retail Store Design:

Peter Grimshaw, Sr. VP Retail, Franklin Quest

Graphics:

Franklin Quest Creative Services Department

SUCCESSORIES

Celex Group, Inc.
Lombard, Illinois

Step inside a Successories store, and it feels like you have just gained access to "the boardroom".

This specialty retailer creates and sells motivational materials: books, tapes, apparel, executive organizational elements, plaques, posters and cards. Everything in the store has one common thread: to help customers reach their individual goals — whether personal or professional.

In line with the concept of promoting positive attitudes and thoughts, the environment of the store has been designed to project a high-achiever image. Cherry wood, with a deep stain, is used in combination with dark laminates in a faux green patina. Display units and fixtures are fabricated to convey a corporate attitude.

Successories' motto, "Our goal is to help you reach yours" is more than just a slogan; it has been incorporated as an integral part of their design identity. Customers first notice the motto at the storefront in conjunction with the company's logo. The motto is also printed on all shopping bags and collateral. Since "success" posters are a major merchandise category, special poster tubes have been designed featuring the Successories logo and motto.

Successories' foray into the retail store arena comes on the heels of their well-established catalog operation. Without losing a beat, they've taken their merchandise line and the philosophy behind it, and translated it effectively through an integrated design program (from store to selling materials) that restates their mission and reinforces their very unique image.

Architecture and Interior Store Design: *Tony L. Horton, T L Horton Design, Inc., Dallas, TX*
Collateral Graphics: *Celex Group, Inc., Lombard, IL*
Photographer: *Joe Aker, Aker Photography*

COMPUTER CITY

A Division of Tandy Corporation, Fort Worth, Texas

The big yellow triangle points to "the city" — Computer City. It is an ultra-simple graphic and it is used to its absolute maximum to express the bigness of this computer superstore.

It all starts on the store facade where the word "city" appears, unfettered, across the golden triangle in an unabashed urban scrawl.

From there on, the graphics are utterly consistent, with the triangle translated into arrows throughout the store's interior — pointing to the enormous selection of computers and computer software that are on display. What might ordinarily be an overwhelming shopping expedition becomes easy and comfortable, thanks to the excellent signage and smart graphics.

The easily recognizable logo is everywhere: on all stationery, labeling and packaging as well as on preferred customer cards. With quick identity and well-designed store layout, Computer City delivers a top-of-the-mind awareness to its computer-literate audience.

Retail Store Concept and Graphics: *Computer City Store Planning, Fort Worth, TX*

Byte calls itself The Computer Store and it definitely looks the part. Strong graphic design makes an effective statement about the store's leadership in the field of selling high-tech products. It is modern. It is dynamic. It presents a broad range of products, technical support and consumer information. The store is all of these things. And consumers "receive" the message through a bold and striking identity program which successfully communicates the personality and authority of Byte.

Color, type style and a strong, dominant logo are the devices used as the main elements to establish the Byte identity. Blue and yellow were chosen as the two main colors to convey both authority and warmth. And these colors have been carried through the interior design, in-store graphics and even as detailing on furniture.

Probably the most exciting — and most obvious characteristic is the Byte logo, itself. The exterior of the store is a customer's first encounter with the Byte logo… and the striking facade cannot be missed. Forceful, simple and very inviting.

The capital "B" of Byte has been designed so it can stand alone within a bright yellow circle to form a distinctive branding device which is used extensively on virtually everything. There is hardly a single item that a customer might hold in his hand that lacks the Byte identity — and that applies to the packaging, the catalog, the shopping bag, uniforms and the company's stationery.

By establishing its very distinctive graphic identity, Byte has (along with its commitment to merchandising and service) become a formidable competitor in hi-tech retailing.

Design Consultancy:
RSCG Conran Design, London, England
Photography:
Nicholas Gentilli

SPACE TRADERS

Space Center, Houston, Texas

Space may be the final frontier, but Space Traders at the Space Center Houston is the ultimate in a retail translation of the wonders of what NASA has wrought!

Space Traders retail store is located directly off the central public core at the Visitors' Center at Space Center Houston. As NASA put it, "the marching orders" were to resist the Hollywood impulse and, instead, to create an environment that authentically and dramatically represented the experience of space travel. The format was to be educational: and even the merchandise assembled for sale was to meet strict standards of quality.

Approaching the store the customer is drawn in by a very dynamic Delta wing ceiling which sets the stage for the intergalactic atmosphere. Powerful visual displays are located at the storefront and throughout the store. The layout of the shop subtly controls the flow of customers through space. The departments are set up as boutiques — each with its own space identification. Books are found in the Data Bank. Stationery is on the Launch Pad. Gifts are at the Stardust Gallery and Little Dipper is for kids.

Black and grey are used to communicate the infinity of space with accents of authentic NASA blue. Lighting and light fixtures play an important role in theatrically conveying the space environment. The strong contemporary Space Trader logo and graphics are used consistently everywhere — on display signs and flags, shopping bags, counter displays.

Since customers covet gift merchandise with the words "Space Center", a correlated logo was created — and it appears on everything from sweatshirts to mugs, caps to coveralls. Salespeople (called "crew members") don the coveralls, adding one more element of visual identity in the successful graphic integration of this out-of-the-world retail center.

Design: *John P.Sunderland, Sunderland Innerspace Design, Vancouver, B.C. Canada*
Graphics: *Host Marriott Merchandise Staff*
Photographer: *Mark Milroy*
Visual Display: *Everett Elizade, Host Marriott Merchandise Staff*

THE GAME KEEPER

Goleta, California

In Alice in Wonderland, the Queen believed in impossible things — thinking up "as many as six impossible things before breakfast".

At The Game Keeper, the design team surely encountered twice as many impossible obstacles as Her Highness in their endeavor to create a game store with a totally distinctive identity of its own.

Fact is, The Game Keeper has enthroned its own Queen — a reincarnation of the familiar face one finds in a deck of cards. She peers out at passing shoppers — high atop her vantage point at the store entrance. More times than not, she is dimensional — aggressively popping out to engage attention and encourage customers to step inside.

Besides the Queen, a variety of animated game imagery is employed to set an atmosphere of fun — everything from scrabble pieces to chess sets to darts and dartboards.

Colors are as playful as the images — with black and white (often checkerboarded) accented by clear red and gold.

Movement and energy are inherent in all elements of store design and store collateral. Even the name/logo itself always seems to be performing some kind of stunt. Sometimes its half vertical, half horizontal. And sometimes, it appears in a state of free-fall.

Though there are no mechanical, electrical gimmicks, Game Keeper stores always convey a feeling of animation. Such innovative design makes customers feel more like participants in the "games" than merely lookers. This wonderful whimsy is the attitude that has successfully achieved a high level of image and identity for this unique game emporium.

Architect: *Dan Freund, Perkins Freund Partnership, Beverly Hills, CA*
Store Design: *Janet Perkins, Perkins Freund Partnership, Beverly Hills, CA*
Photographers: *Keith Meyers, Janet Perkins, Dan Freund*

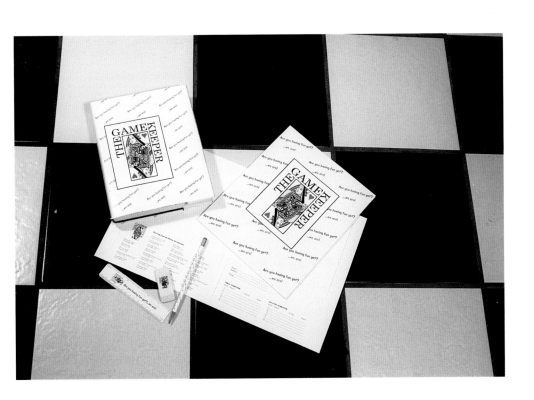

Interior Design and Retail Graphics: Fitch, Inc., Columbus, OH

Webster's dictionary gives a choice of definitions for the word "too". It means "also" and it means "more". There is clearly nothing "also" about the Too Corporation and its stores. This extraordinarily unique retailer, however, does demonstrate an image and identity that is definitely consistent with "more".

Famous for supplying Japanese designers with art and design materials and services, the company is clearly dealing with a target consumer who is aesthetic, sophisticated and part of Japan's visual arts culture. Coming into play was a well-articulated philosophy — one that committed the company to look to the future and to anticipate requirements of designers by providing the most advanced technologies. From these mental gymnastics emerged the name .TOO. (The period before the name explains that everything else existed before that period; and then, beyond that period comes .TOO.)

Though this intellectual philosophy may seem subtle, the ultimate rendering of visual identity is not. It is clear, simple, concise. Shapes are blocked boldly. Storefronts are truly shopper-stoppers. The vocabulary of visual elements repeats the .TOO identity everywhere — on merchandise packaging, shopping bags, calling cards, all environmental graphics, signage and in-store display. And .TOO's persona penetrates people's consciousness even miles from the stores; the whimsical .TOO cars and delivery trucks move the message proclaiming the undeniable originality of this innovative retail image.

ZEBRA

Sunnydale, California

What could be a better metaphor for black and white printing and facsimiles than "Zebra"? How clever of this retailer to adopt this image and then maximize it to set it apart, totally, from its competitors.

By the time the creative owners of this 8-chain store and their collaborative designers completed their comprehensive identity package, it was hard for a customer to visit a zoo without making the mental connection.

The pattern of black and white stripings sets the main design theme for the stores. Even the typography of the Zebra logo is styled with stripes. Accents of bright red add to the crispness of the look. Everywhere, the Zebra graphic pops up. Fuzzy stuffed toy Zebras greet customers. A whimsical striped mailbox invites customer opinions. There are Zebra canvas totes, T-shirts, mugs, water bottles, a stunning wall calendar and a monthly newsletter titled "Zebra Tales." These items are routinely given to customers (as promotions, incentives, good-will gifts) with the purpose of maintaining awareness and generating ongoing business. Packaging, packing boxes, price lists and stationery continue the identity.

Since customers include corporations as well as walk-in clientele, Zebra Copy provides its own delivery service. Recognizing this as yet another opportunity to flaunt their equine identity, the company's "horsepower" includes a fleet of trucks that are Zebra-camouflaged!

In a proliferating copy-store industry, Zebra Copy has succeeded in achieving individuality and establishing itself as a top-of-the-mind choice for consumers.

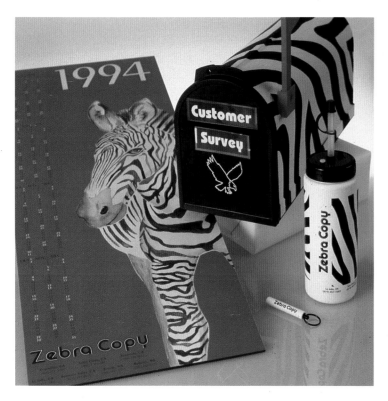

Architect: *James Dumas and Associates, Santa Clara, CA*
Store Concept, Graphics and Design: *Andy, Jamie and Sidney Kerr*
Photographer: *Kim Hoogner, Infinity Color*

INDEX BY RETAIL IDENTITY

INDEX BY ARCHITECTURAL AND DESIGN FIRMS